Go To B

The Story of Firefi... in Portsmouth

PETER SMITH

Down Memory Lane I linger long,
Till evening shadows fall,
To dream of golden days bygone,
And radiant hours recall.

MILESTONE PUBLICATIONS

Phototypesetting by The Monitor.
66 Station Road, Hayling Island, Hampshire
Printed in Great Britain by
Conifer Press, Fareham, Hampshire

Published by Milestone Publications
62 Murray Road, Horndean, Hants PO8 9JL

British Library Cataloguing in Publication Data

Smith, Peter
   Go to blazes : the history of firefighting
   in Portsmouth.   (Down memory lane, 19)
   1. Fire extinction   England   Portsmouth
   (Hampshire)   History 2. Portsmouth
   (Hampshire)   History
   I. Title II. Series
   628.9′25′09422792   TH9539.P6

ISBN 0-903852-89-6

One of Portsmouth's Merryweather steam fire engines at Southsea.

(Pamlin prints)

In Portsmouth's three fire stations lights stabbed the darkness and the night silence was shattered by sudden activity as the city's firefighters swung their machines out into the deserted streets. In the heart of Southsea a large disused hospital was ablaze, flames shooting from its ground floor windows, dense smoke pouring from its upper floors. It was 1.25 a.m. on March 27, 1974. Portsmouth City Fire Brigade was engaged on its last big fire in the city. Four days later it went out of existence on becoming part of the new all-Hampshire county brigade. One era in the history of how Portsmouth has protected itself against fire had ended – and another had begun.

Portsmouth, an island city and major naval port since the days of the Romans, went through its greatest ordeals by fire when the nation was at war – at the hands of the French who came by sea in the Thirteenth Century, and at the hands of the Germans from the air in the Twentieth Century.

Ever since the late 1400's when Portsmouth was made a military and naval port, with a military responsibility for dealing with the inherent fire risks, the city has been protected by a great variety of fire-fighting forces operating in various combinations. Over the Centuries, military, parish, industrial, volunteer, police, auxiliary, national and municipal fire brigades have served the city which is now in the hands of Hampshire Fire Brigade, which was formed in 1974.

But long before the people of Portsmouth had any form of fire brigade or knew anything of fire-fighting they learned of the catastrophe that fire could bring. In the Thirteenth and Fourteenth Centuries it was their fate to see the destruction of Portsmouth by fire seven times in 120 years – nearly every time under the torches of the French, with whom England was at war.

In 1265 the inhabitants of Portsmouth first experienced the French sailing to their shores, landing and burning the town down. Scarcely had they recovered from the ordeal, before, in the following year, the town was burned again – this time by Englishmen. This was maritime revenge for the son of the Earl of Leicester. Simon de Montford, who had led a gang of pirates out of the Cinque Ports in the eastern passages of the English Channel. To combat his plundering of any passing ship a small fleet set sail against him and, capturing some of his ships, hanged several of his pirates. In revenge, he gathered his remaining men and left for Portsmouth, landing on November 25, 1266, when he set fire to the whole town.

Twice in two years the people of Portsmouth had seen their town burned. But these fires were just a prelude to what was to befall their grand-children less than 100 years later. For the inhabitants alive in the 50 years between 1336 and 1386 saw the destruction of the port by the French six times.

After the invader had repeated the fiery ordeal and destroyed the town for the last time in 1386, it is not surprising that an historian later wrote a little ruefully, "such was the weak state of the national defence that there appears to have been neither men nor ships to oppose them."

About 100 years later, in the latter half of the Fifteenth Century, King Henry VII decided to build his Royal Dockyard and storehouses in Portsmouth, and from that date the city became an increasingly important naval and military base.

One notable feature of its history was that it became the scene of a series of massive conflagrations from three military sources – from within the Dockyard walls; from the military installations in Southsea Castle and at Point; and from the warships in and around the harbour. From the earliest days, the hazards of ship fires in and around Portsmouth were multiplied by the military nature of the vessels and the armaments they carried. After once being bombarded by cannon-balls from a burning vessel at Spithead when her loaded guns went off, the residents of Old Portsmouth were known to flee when wooden warships of old provided the same threat in subsequent fires.

Right from the start the Navy's storehouses inside the Dockyard were enormous buildings packed with great quantities of highly flammable materials, which, once on fire, produced great consternation in the town itself.

The first such ordeal which the contemporary writers called a "disaster to Portsmouth" occurred on June 17, 1557, when the storehouses on the north side of what was known as King Street went up in flames.

Before it was over, the Navy's principle beer warehouse, containing 87 tons of casked beer had been destroyed with 95,000 pints of beer lost, together with the main cooper's working house next door where 100 tons of empty casks, plus all the tools and equipment were also destroyed.

Less than 20 years later, King Street was the scene of an even more disastrous conflagration, so bad that two nationwide collections were authorized by Elizabeth I's Government to provide for the "distressed" inhabitants of Portsmouth. On August 4, 1576 the fire, which started in the Navy storehouses, destroyed them and swept into the nearby dwelling houses. Most of the Dockyard was burned down and the loss was said at the time to be in excess of £2,200 – a sum so great that the people of Portsmouth "were not able of themselves to recover the same."

Early in the 1600's the city began waking up to the dangers. After 1609 you could get landed with a hefty fine if your chimney was still smoking at night, and a smaller fine if you had an accidental chimney fire by day. Every thatched roof round the Dockyard was replaced by tiles, and all buildings within 40 feet of the Dockyard were knocked down anyway. When a drunken Portsea woman set herself on fire and died in 1664 the authorities breathed a sigh of relief that she had narrowly missed staggering into a Dockyard warehouse. They promptly went out and bought a fire engine for £20.

While these precautions were being taken around the Dockyard, the fire hazard from the second source – Southsea Castle – raised its ugly head. In March, 1626, the Castle caught fire for the first time, causing great panic among the ships moored off the beach. Several ran aground in their haste to escape what was feared would be a huge explosion. But none came as the Castle was not stocked with arms or powder at the time. Its timber structure collapsed, and the Castle burned to the ground. In 1640 a second great fire broke out in the Castle, again in March, and this time its lodging rooms and store rooms for ammunition and provisions were destroyed.

Then it was the turn of the ships to bring more fire hazards to the port. Of all the ways fire can strike the most terrible is with a fire on board ship – and Portsmouth, with its maritime heritage has known this awful menace repeatedly through the Centuries.

Most prominent feature of such fires in the Seventeenth, Eighteenth and Nineteenth Centuries was the lack of effective fire-fighting facilities afloat. Once fire took hold of the wooden warships they nearly always burned to the water. Earliest recorded loss of a warship by fire in Portsmouth was the Pelican, a 38-gun ship built in 1650, and burned out in an accidental fire at Portsmouth six years later.

Not all ship fires of that time were accidental. Customs men would set fire to smuggling ships deliberately – like the collier found with brandy and tea under her coal in 1767, and a sloop, both of which were burned at Blockhouse Point.

But Portsmouth hardly needed the Customs to light its fires. The latter half of the 1700's were disastrous for the port with dreadful fires occurring in all sections of the town. By far the worst of the fires to strike Southsea Castle came when it was in full military use.

On August 23, 1759, 17 men, women and children were killed in an explosion and fire that damaged the Castle so badly it was never completely repaired. A regiment commanded by the Duke of Richmond stored its powder and ammunition in the Castle's east

The burning of the Boyne, the man o'war which blazed off Southsea in 1795. (See page 5).

Courtesy The News

wing. Women were blamed for the fire. It was reckoned they let sparks from their furze fire fall down through the cracks in the floor onto the powder below. The explosion blew up the east wing, and blew open the doors to the magazine in the west wing – but luckily it never went up. Sixteen people died instantly, and one more died after being removed from the ruins.

A year later came the first of three more disastrous fires in the Dockyard each of which in turn almost destroyed it. Lightning during a thunderstorm on July 3, 1760 hit one of the principle warehouses in the 'Yard, starting an immense fire which burned it and another of the largest warehouses down. They contained huge quantities of pitch, tar, oil, turpentine and dry stores, and the loss was put at £40,000.

But in 1770 a conflagration worse than any seen before not only razed most of the Dockyard and threatened Portsmouth itself, but prompted a contemporary writer to describe it as of "so tremendous a character as almost to threaten the extinction of our Naval power."

On July 27, at low tide, when the Dockyard slept, and in the most inaccessible place, the fire was started, it was suspected, deliberately. Large warehouses and the pitch and tar stores were the first mighty buildings to be consumed. Temporary sheds caught fire and spread the flames to the spinning houses. Swiftly the conflagration swept through the oarhouse, carpenters warehouse and the mast house, which were quickly destroyed, wiping out enough ropes, masts and sails to have fully equipped at least 30 men o' war.

At this stage every section of the Dockyard had suffered some damage, and just as the residents began to fear for the whole of Portsmouth, came salvation. The wind changed direction.

With Dockyard personnel and seamen attacking the fires with water and sand, and with some buildings demolished as fire breaks the great blaze was controlled, though its hot spots smouldered for five weeks. Unknown political saboteurs were blamed – thought possibly to be French. A £1,000 reward was offered by the Admiralty for the arsonist, but without result.

They had better luck in 1776 when they caught the next fire-raiser, who confessed and was publicly hanged in view of the ruins he had caused. "Jack the Painter" was how the poets immortalized him, but he usually answered to the name James Hill, or Hind, or Aitkens.

On December 7 he intended to wipe out the entire Dockyard but had to be content with the desctruction of the Round House, and a few singed warehouses. Damp matches were his downfall. His master plan was to fire some houses in the town – then, with the engines engaged, light up the Dockyard. But only one of his fires took hold because of those matches, and enough evidence remained to trap him. They hanged him from the mizzen mast of the frigate Arethusa, then took down his body and suspended it in chains at Blockhouse Point at the harbour entrance. But it didn't stay there long. Sailors used the bones to settle a drinking debt at a Gosport pub.

Within two years it was the turn of Point and Southsea to suffer a series of frightening fires. In 1778 and 1782, two large fires razed rows of houses on The Hard, Portsea – the 1778 blaze carrying with it an omen of evil. For on the site where the houses stood the Keppels Head, a large house was built. On April 25, 1803 it too was destroyed by fire.

You could say that the people of the Point only got what they deserved. In 1704, punishment was laid down for those who indulged in "annointing rats with turpentine and setting them on fire" – not because of the "abominable cruelty", but through fear that the blazing rodents might set fire to the Navy's magazines or residents' houses.

In this same series of fires in the late 1700's was one in 1794 in Battery Row which had an historically important effect on the fire-fighting of the day. After the blaze, the church reacted by forming a

Jack the Painter, Dockyard arsonist of 1776. (See page 4).

parish fire brigade – and they had a neat way of encouraging "activity in the firemen". The firemen on the first engine to arrive would get a guinea each – but if the neighbouring parish beat them there, its firemen would get two guineas. Every resident had to keep two leather buckets handy for fire-fighting, and the church agreed to pay water cart drivers for every cart load they carried to any fire.

The 1790's was one of the worst ever decades for ship fires around Portsmouth, frightening the residents of Point and Southsea, and resulting in the loss of two British men o' war, two merchant ships, and a captured French ship in separate fires. First ship lost was the French prize, the Impetueux, which caught fire in Portsmouth Harbour on August 29, 1790 after a gunpowder accident on board. Seven men trapped below decks died in the spreading inferno which panicked many Portsmouth residents into fleeing the town, fearing that the blaze would spread to the powder magazines near her moorings – but this time it didn't.

Next time it did. When the 98-gun man o' war, Boyne caught fire eight months later on May 1, 1795, the fears that caused the panic before, came true.

As the ship blazed at Spithead her loaded guns went off in a continual two-hour cannonade. Worse was to come. Her cables burned through, she grounded off Southsea Castle and her magazines exploded, showering Southsea with shrapnel, shot and blazing debris. Of 750 men on board, 14 were lost.

Before the turn of the Century three more ships were lost in the worst single year of all – 1799. On November 9, two merchant vessels caught fire and were lost inside Portsmouth Harbour and another warship, the H.M.S. Prince Frederick, a 64-gunner, was destroyed in a blaze at Spithead.

Then came catastrophe. All the anxieties over the presence of the military at Point were justified by one mighty explosion on June 24, 1809. Had it not been so tragic, with more than 30 men, women and children killed, and with widespread devastation, it would have been comic. It was a woman's fault again. Remember the drunken woman who nearly burned down the Dockyard, and the women who blew up Southsea Castle. This time, would you believe, it was a dear old soul from Portsea.

On the beach at Point the 2nd Battalion of the 8th Regiment of Foot had just disembarked its ammunition and powder, when along she came. A pipe-smoking woman. Yes, you've guessed it. She knocked out her pipe on a barrel of gunpowder – and in the blast nearly every pane of glass in Point was shattered, many roofs were blown off, fires started, and panic generated. Brave soldiers and sailors rolled more gunpowder kegs away from the flames but one huge store was set ablaze. And what do you think? Surrounded by death and destruction, the old woman of Portsea lived. A barrel landed over her head and protected her from the spreading flames.

In 1827 Portsmouth experienced its first big ship blaze inside the Dockyard, all previous ship fires being afloat in the harbour or at sea. H.M.S. Diamond, a frigate back from South America for a refit, caught fire on February 13. The guns of H.M.S. Victory were fired rapidly to raise the alarm and soon the ship's crew and Dockyardmen were fighting the blaze. They worked in vain and, fanned by a strong breeze, the flames spread until she burned out.

Ten years later on October 27, 1837 came the first of three large fire disasters at sea around Portsmouth. The Colonist – en route from London to Barbados – got no further than the Mother Bank in the Solent, where she caught fire. She was quickly beyond saving and for 27 hours the people of Portsmouth watched the nautical bonfire. When she had burned out, she was towed to Haslar Beach and smouldered to her grave.

Probably the worst maritime fire disaster in Spithead's historic marine roadstead was the blaze on June 3, 1859 that burned out the Eastern Monarch, a 1,700-ton transport ship from the Indies. She

had on board 352 soldiers, mainly Crimean and Indian war veterans and invalids, 30 women and 53 children. Ten people were killed when she was hit by a violent explosion. A vast rescue operation saved everyone else before a series of explosions blew the ship apart, leaving her to settle on the Arrow Bank and burn out.

Last of the big wooden vessels to provide a fiery spectacle at Spithead was the 654-ton merchantman, Ocean Home. In 1869 she sheltered with other vessels from a violent storm when fire broke out amid her cargo of compressed hay. The fire was unstoppable and to eliminate the danger to other ships, she was beached off Haslar and scuttled, her remains joining those of the Colonist.

Meanwhile in the town in 1836, for the first time ever, the responsibility for protecting Portsmouth from fire shifted from volunteer and parish brigades plus whatever military assistance could be begged, to the shoulders of the police under the surveillance of the Watch Committee. From February 8, 1836, when the Watch Committee was formed, until 1938, when the Auxiliary Fire Service was formed, the Portsmouth Borough Police Fire Brigade had sole responsibility for fire coverage in the town – which brought a Century of chequered history.

The police brigade ceased to exist in August 1941 when, together with the Auxiliary Fire Service, it was taken over as part of the National Fire Service. During the 100 years prior to World War II it dealt with 44 major fires.

Its individual chief officers were regarded as some of the finest firemen in Britain, but the system of protecting Portsmouth was nationally regarded as inefficient by the fire service and the general public alike. Things were bad elsewhere but Portsmouth was reckoned by the official national journal of the fire service to be the worst. Year after year, together with the local press, it warned that there was near "criminal neglect" of fire cover in the city. But no-one listened. Every time a serious blaze raged in Portsmouth and the woefully inadequate borough police brigade had to be bailed out by the military, the critics tutted "we told you so". Each disaster brought forward a new public outcry and another warning, but when the shouting had died down, nothing was done.

It got off to a bad start from day one, as the engines it inherited from the various parishes were already in need of repair – and as late as 1934 the position had not improved. So what was this system which the Watch Committee approved, the fire service ridiculed, and which quite simply failed?

The brigade consisted of a small nucleus of "policemen-firemen" who were police officers who would turn out and man the first engine to answer a call, with the remainder of the police force theoretically being sent on to provide further assistance if necessary. It was argued that this gave the town a very large brigade. Practical difficulties, however dictated otherwise.

From the start the Watch Committee knew well the problems. Take the engines. Handed over by the Portsmouth parish churchwardens in 1837, they were soon found to be "next to useless". Providing water supplies was another problem – one which proved fatal at a terrible fire 30 years later when seven people died. Farlington and Portsea Waterworks companies were prepared to give Watch Committee members keys to the water mains, and the grand sum of £5 was set aside for equipment towards better water supplies. Already there was unrest among the general public. After several fires in 1838 a volunteer brigade was formed at Landport and a fire insurance company provided the fire engine.

By 1850 the engines used by the borough police brigade were a laughing stock. Portsea's was "condemned as worn out and entirely unfit." Landport's didn't work at a big blaze, and by the time the military engines arrived, they were too late to help.

At last, the message filtered through and in 1853 Portsmouth bought its own fire-engine for the police. It was soon used. On September 29, 1853 a serious blaze broke out in an unfinished villa opposite Windsor Terrace, Southsea. The new engine was drawn

One of Portsmouth's manual fire-engines of 1850.

Courtesy James Cramer

from its Spring Street station by two horses borrowed from an omnibus. Two villas were destroyed, but after 45 minutes working, the engine saved the rest of the street.

There was a basic fault in the belief that the town could safely rely on military fire-engines for immediate assistance. Each garrison commander stood to face a court-martial if fire broke out on his establishment while his engine was out assisting the town. Hence, in most cases, he would wait until a fire was well under way before committing his engine to help.

Portsmouth was without an escape ladder until the 1860's when five awful fires – three inside a year – spurred the authorities into providing this much needed piece of equipment.

First, on March 8, 1861, Cooke's Circus provided a spectacular blaze in Buckingham Street and Chandos Street. The Landport engine was supported by one of the Dockyard engines, with further military assistance coming from the engines of the Royal Engineers 11th Regiment and 19th Regiment. Despite their efforts, the circus was reduced to ashes with nine houses devoured as the conflagration spread. Five more homes were damaged and eight of the circus horses perished. Damage was estimated at £5,000.

Then came the three fires in the space of 12 months. On January 2, 1863 fire broke out in a house in College Street, Portsea and with an inadequate water supply and no escape ladder, the firemen could not reach a mother and six children on the top floor. All seven perished. Too late, an inquest jury recommended that an escape ladder be purchased.

Six days later the Mile End Mills went up in flames. Inadequate equipment again meant that the police brigade could not reach the fire – and only the arrival of the Royal Marine Artillery engine prevented a major outbreak. The mill was burned out and nearby houses damaged.

An even greater blaze razed Pike's Brewery in Penny Street on January 11, 1864 and once again the borough brigade was quickly overpowered by the fire which threatened the nearby jail. Only a massive amount of military support from the Dockyard, Cambridge Barracks, Fort Cumberland, and sailors from ships in Harbour summoned by the firing of H.M.S. Victory's guns, saved the day. The only good to come from these fires was that Portsmouth got its escape ladder and from that time onwards it was always reasonably equipped with appliances.

But still the authorities never appreciated the need for men. In the fifth big fire of the 1860's, on June 30, 1868, the Kings Mills, which dated from 1714, burned down. As usual, the borough's engines were supported by military engines with the Gunwharf machine figuring

prominently. Damage was another £4,000.

Three large fires which wiped out two coaching inns and another brewery continued to test the borough's fire-fighters early in the 1870's before another full-scale conflagration inside the Dockyard showed where the even greater threat rested.

On May 7, 1807 the Blue Posts, Broad Street, which was the town's principle coaching house dating from 1613, was burned to the ground despite the efforts of the borough's engines backed up by the Royal Artillery 46th Regiment. Later in the same year, on October 2 it was the turn of the Coach and Horses Inn, Hilsea to be turned to rubble. This time the engine of the 11th Brigade, Royal Artillery did good work. The Brunswick Brewery, Grigg Street was burned out in a blaze on March 29, 1872.

Portsmouth's principle coaching house, the Blue Posts in Broad Street, burned down in 1870. (See page 8).

Yet still the Dockyard provided the greatest threat and the sweeping, raging blaze on January 15, 1874 proved the point. When the West Sea Store, an enormous warehouse of three floors with an attic and a basement caught fire from top to bottom, the residents of Portsmouth really feared that the whole 'Yard was doomed.

Packed in the warehouse were chairs, carpets, matting, blankets, curtains, leather, glass, china, rope, furniture and valuable articles like telescopes, while the cellar and attic housed lumber and drums of oil. When the alarm was raised, 16 engines from the military barracks, the Dockyard and the borough, manned by firemen, sailors and soldiers massed in response to the Red Ensign being flown upside down from the foremast of the Duke of Wellington (the fire signal). Together they saved the ground floor of the building. More than 30 men were injured and the loss was put at £30,000. Three years later, on January 11, 1877 another of the 'Yard's great stores was burned to the ground.

On the other side of the Dockyard wall the terrible lessons were still not being learned. In 1878 came the first of seven more huge fires which levelled three theatres, another circus, another inn, a mission chapel, and which brought death to highlight the continuing failure of the system.

Firstly, on September 13, 1878 a fire which broke out in the old Blue Bell Theatre burned it out, swept on through Tilley's soap factory, which was also lost, and was eventually stopped only after damaging an adjoining boarding school. The battle to stop the flames brought in engines from the Royal Artillery, 55th Regiment and 109th Regiment, the Royal Engineers and the Army Service Corps.

When the next inferno swept through Bow Street, Landport on April 1, 1882 – the first of three big fires in five weeks – even more military fire-fighters were called in to tackle it. It started in Ginnetts Circus which was reduced to a charred skeleton. As the engines were overwhelmed, the fire swept on through four houses in Surrey Street,

A Portsmouth police fireman leads out the horses for the engines, about 1890.
Courtesy James Cramer

9

and damaged seven others, finally reaching the railway station.

The borough's engine was supported by four others – a Dockyard steamer, the Anglesea Barracks manual, the Harbour Station manual and the Clarence Barracks engine. To operate the manuals men were drawn in from the Metropolitan Police, the 92nd Gordon Highlanders, the 17th Leicestershire Regiment, the 73rd Black Watch and the Royal Marine Artillery before the spreading flames were contained.

This fire caused the considerable loss of £2,450 but worse was to follow. When the Prince's Theatre in Lake Road, Landport was left a blackened shell in a blaze on April 25, damage was estimated at £4,550. This time the borough engine and the machine of the Gordon Highlanders held the fire. Scarcely two weeks had passed when, on May 6 the King's Head Inn at Hilsea caught fire. The borough's engine worked alongside the Hilsea Barracks manual, but they could not save the building from destruction.

Out of the ashes of the old Blue Bell Theatre rose Bernard's Amphitheatre, which 12 years later became the next casualty. It was the scene of a devastating fire on December 25, 1890, causing the huge loss of £17,000. Borough and Dockyard steamers fought the Christmas blaze together.

A year later in a dreadful fatal fire the failings of the police system almost certainly cost two lives. On Saturday nights most constables were already busy on their beats – and it took longer than usual to round up enough men even to man skeleton crews for the engines. When a drapers store at 119, Commercial Road burst into flames on Saturday, March 28, 1891 it took 20 minutes to get the machines to the scene – and by that time it was too late for two people who perished in the fire. This time the inquest jury said, "the force of police at disposal for fire brigade purposes is deplorably inadequate."

Later the same year the two borough steamers were again unable to save the Zenana Mission Chapel in Kent Street, and it was razed

at a loss of £4,000.

Yet 1891 was a significant year for it saw the appointment of the first of five chief fire officers, who in turn proved to be the brigade's greatest assets, all drawing the highest possible praise from within the fire service. In 1891 Superintendent Arthur Pordage took command. He reorganized the brigade and quickly improved its efficiency.

After four years he moved to become the chief officer of the Edinburgh Fire Brigade, where he continued a long and distinguished career. While he was in Portsmouth he was responsible for the appointment of the man who succeeded him in commanding the brigade.

This was Superintendent Harry Vassie who began his fire service career with the Metropolitan Fire Brigade in London in 1881. He rose through the ranks until he became drill instructor at Southwark ten years later. He left to become engineer to Pordage's new brigade in Portsmouth in 1891, and when Pordage left, Vassie filled the vacancy – a position he held with great success from 1895 until 1910.

Yet even under these two great men, Portsmouth's brigade was held to ridicule by the fire service. At the turn of the Century a national fire service magazine featured the Portsmouth brigade, and was forced to highlight its dreadful short-comings.

A special correspondent for the magazine visited the "after-thought" fire station, which in itself was reckoned to be one of the worst wooden fire risks in the town. He found a horsed escape and two antiquated steamers, one of which took half-an-hour to get up steam, and a force consisting of 16 men, three coachmen and an assistant engineer. Some force! He found none of the town's large buildings were directly linked to the station and there was not one automatic fire alarm anywhere.

An effort was made to improve the appliances in 1900 when the brigade received a new first-aid machine with a 55-foot ladder, and a

Superintendent Arthur Pordage, in charge at Portsmouth from 1891 - 1896. (See page 10).

horsed hose-tender and sliding carriage, costing £160 from Messrs. E.A. Bailey & Co. Ltd.

With the brigade at its lowest ebb the first two years of the 1900's brought two more frightening fires. On December 8, 1901 the magnificent Queen's Hotel, Southsea caught fire. Engines from the Dockyard and Victoria Barracks assisted the borough's hard-pressed machines, but the grand hotel was lost. Tragically, two chambermaids perished in the flames. Then, in September 1902 Reed and Creebull's timber yard – a constant source of fear to the residents of River Street, Portsea – went up in flames. Predictably the whole yard was destroyed and several nearby houses badly damaged.

Portsmouth, now with a population of 190,000 people, again reacted to the public outcries caused by these fires, and heeding the numerous warnings of impending fiery doom, chose to buy a new engine.

This time, as befitting a town the size of Portsmouth, it was decreed that a civic reception, with pomp and ceremony, should fanfare the arrival of the new Merryweather self-propelled steamer on July 18, 1903. It was to be paraded in its shining glory to the civic dignitaries in a Guildhall Square demonstration. It made a triumphal entry, "brass gleaming and smoke pouring from its funnel in a stirring manner". Its exit wasn't quite so triumphal. Turning into the square its wheels jammed in a tram line, and the assembled dignitaries had a grandstand view of their much-heralded engine crashing in a spectacular cloud of steam and smoke. The remains were ignominiously towed away for repair.

But a year later it had been mended, and was there on July 19, 1904 when South Parade Pier went up in flames. From what was saved of the pier, a new edifice, the dominant feature of Southsea seafront, was built. This lasted for 70 years until it provided a film-maker's perfect dream fire, and blazed to destruction before assembled and well-prepared film cameras.

Portsmouth horse-drawn fire-engine outside the fire station about 1900.

Portsmouth horse-drawn ladders in 1912.

On parade with Portsmouth's self-propelled steamer at the Guildhall in 1912.

Portsmouth's motor escape in 1912 with "Chief" John Ogburn (right). (See page 13).

All these fires were overshadowed by a tremendous holocaust on January 2, 1907 when the enormous Camp Store Block in the Gunwharf burned in a monstrous spectacular outbreak that was fought for hours in vain by four Dockyard steamers, both the borough steamers and its horsed escape. When the debris was sifted it was found that damage to the almost unimaginable total of £250,000 had been caused.

A month later, 300 people were thrown out of work when the stay factory of L. Reynolds and Co. Ltd. caught fire in Cannon Street, Landport on February 3. The borough's steamer, its new motorized engine and horsed escape managed to save half the building from destruction.

In 1908 it was the turn of the Landport Drapery Bazaar to suffer. This huge department store was struck by lightning on December 22, and the resultant fire severely damaged the building. By an unhappy coincidence, December 22 was the date 57 years later in 1965 when the store was again ravaged by fire.

1909 had its moments. In October, the Courage Works at Southsea were razed in a £5,000 blaze, and at this time the brigade was about to get a new chief fire officer who matched the reputation of the two men who had gone before him. Superintendent John G. Ogburn took command in 1910, a choice that surprised no-one by all accounts. Fire magazine said at the time that he was a man "destined to become chief of the brigade from early in his career". As a sergeant at the turn of the Century he was a versatile chap – "a handyman, police sergeant, second officer of the brigade, engineer, police photographer, and capable of 101 other jobs" was how they viewed him. He went on to take charge of the brigade until 1919, and he died in Portsmouth on April 19, 1930.

Ogburn made great progress in the field of training works brigades. Officials at the Portsmouth Workhouse demonstrated the value of his practical training when an oil fire broke out in the kitchen of the workhouse. The Workhouse Union Fire Brigade

Getting steamed up! A steamer at work pumping away flood water at Hilsea in December, 1912.   *Courtesy James Cramer*

stopped what might have been a major blaze, helped by the borough brigade, giving Ogburn the satisfaction of seeing how his workhouse pupils had obviously digested his drill instruction.

Under Ogburn in 1912 the brigade's complete list of appliances and equipment was one horse-drawn steamer, one motor escape, one motor hose-and-ladder truck, one horsed escape van, one horse-drawn chemical engine and hose tender, one horse-drawn dog cart with 70-foot ladders, eight hose carts, 12 hand escapes, 17 hand pumps, six chemical engines, 24 jumping sheets, and 9,600 feet of hose. A year later another motor pump was added at a cost of £700.

While the borough brigade continued suffering criticism, the fire-fighting organization within the Dockyard came in for great praise for the way it tackled another massive blaze inside the establishment in 1913. On December 20, the Semaphore Tower and sail loft were destroyed in a colossal fire which killed two men and put the whole 'Yard at risk. Only the resolute fire-fighting of an incredibly large force of 1,000 men, aided once again by a kindly wind direction, saved the day.

Duty watchmen on the battle cruiser Queen Mary raised the alarm, and in response all 15 warships in harbour sent 50 men each, every military barracks in the town sent fire engines. Chief Ogburn took two engines in, and even the Royal Clarence Victualling Yard at Gosport sent a fire-engine over on the floating bridge. Not only was the sail loft packed with highly flammable materials like tarred rope and flag silks, but near the building were seven huge tanks holding 30,000 gallons of oil.

All the 'Yard's most volatile warehouses were upwind which was the only lucky factor of the day. The Queen Mary was removed to safety, and eight steam pumpers played on the southern end of the building to prevent the fire spreading. Two hours into the blaze, the Semaphore Tower, built in 1833, collapsed, toppling into the sea in a ball of flame.

It was later strongly rumoured that the Suffragettes had fired the building in their campaign of that time, or that German saboteurs had been busy — remember, World War I was only a year away.

A grateful editorial in the Evening News thanked the firemen for their "great and unceasing efforts" which saved the 'Yard and the town, and questioned the wisdom of the naval authorities in having wooden warehouses stacked with stores that burned readily, placed near thousands of gallons of oil.

Only after the unstable ruins of the building's walls had been blown down with explosives were the bodies of the two men later recovered. Within weeks, in January 1914, Ogburn and his men were hard-pressed again in the town when fire razed Fry's builders and

Eastney Royal Marine fire-fighters working a manual engine at the Beach Mansions Hotel fire in June, 1913. Courtesy James Cramer

decorators premises at a loss of £4,000.

As had often been the case before, the next serious blaze in the Dockyard during World War I, was reckoned to be a case of arson, but again a reward offered by the Admiralty produced no results. In the fire on January 31, 1915, one large shed in Building Slip Road caught fire. Before it was stopped the fast-spreading flames had taken the roofs off four slips, and two more jetties were destroyed. A year later another war-time fire on January 23, 1916 burned out the 'Yard's electrical shop, this fire again only being halted by the combined efforts of Dockyard and borough firemen.

The advent of World War I caused some parish fire brigades considerable difficulties and resulted, for example, in a plea for help from Cosham Parish Fire Brigade. At this time each parish council was responsible, under the Lighting and Watching Act, for providing "the necessary appliances and men for the purpose of protecting each parish against fire". Calling up men for the war hit

During World War I these Portsmouth Volunteer firemen assisted the police firemen.   *Courtesy James Cramer*

Fire hero. Police Fireman Arthur Croucher earned a medal, certificate and commendation for saving life in a blaze in Marmion Road, Southsea in 1916.   *Courtesy City Records Office*

15

Cosham Parish Fire Brigade so hard that by the spring of 1918 there wasn't a man left.

Pity the poor clerk of Cosham Parish Council, Mr. John Adamson. He sought assistance from the military, writing to the Provost Marshall, Southern Defences, Portsmouth on June 6, 1918.

"The Council has provided the necessary apparatus and the Parish is well provided with hydrants and a good supply of water. Before the war the Brigade had a complement of 12 men but since the war started the number has been steadily decreasing and the last man was recently called up. Therefore the Council is now without men to act as firemen as other suitable civilians cannot be found.

"It is thought by the Council that with your approval the Military Authorities might be able to assist the Council in its serious dilemma by allocating a small number of men from the Hilsea Lines to take charge of our fire appliances and to hold themselves in readiness to cope with any outbreak of fire."

The reply was a gem. The Portsmouth Garrison could offer help – provided Cosham could arrange to have its fires only when the military engine was free, or after 9.30 p.m. at night! But the military would train men right away.

"Immediate steps will be taken to train a few men of the non-combatants corps stationed at Hilsea for this purpose," wrote the Garrison Commander. "Owing to their duties it will not be possible to collect them at short notice during the daytime. They will therefore only be available after 9.30 p.m.

"In the event of a fire by day the military motor fire engine at Hilsea, could, if not at the time engaged, turn out at a moments notice in aid of the civil authorities."

Once the war had passed, the brigade recovered quickly and was drilling again regularly throughout 1919 and into the 1920's. One fire in the brigade's log-book for July, 1920 illustrates its efficiency.

Called to a hay rick ablaze at The Mills, Davey Farm, Purbrook at 7.45 p.m., the brigade had mustered, left the station, arrived, and were at work by 7.55 p.m. on a fire that lasted for four hours.

The end of hostilities brought the return to Portsmouth of maybe the greatest figure in the police brigade history – Superintendent Charles G. Gould. He earned a string of superlatives for his commanding personality which made him a dominant character throughout the British fire service. His naval career was also one of great note, and together they combined to make him a most popular man in the town.

His fame spread from the days of World War I when he was one of only five survivors from the Coronel disaster. On August 2, 1914 he was called out of the town police into the navy and was drafted to H.M.S. Good Hope under the flag of Sir Christopher Craddock.

Chief Petty Officer Gould and four men were landed at Coronel to pick up the position of Admiral Graf Spee's fleet from the shore, but while they were on land, the German fleet chased the British squadron and decimated it. Later, H.M.S. Glasgow retrieved C.P.O. Gould and his men – the lone survivors of the squadron – and enabled them to take part in the great revenge sea battle, the Battle of the Falkland Islands when Graf Spee's fleet was beaten.

After being decorated at Gallipolli he was promoted lieutenant in November 1918, and a year later, at the end of hostilities, he returned to take charge of the Portsmouth Police Fire Brigade. He quickly earned the praise of all. "One of the most Herculean members of the fire service," said one fire magazine, "a man with a profound knowledge of the world's fire brigades having visited a great number of them, and with a proud reputation of being a first-class fire officer with an all-absorbing desire to save human life," said another.

He was appointed to the highest position in the Professional Fire Brigades Association, its president, in March 1928 and served for a year, bringing credit to the Association and upon the shoulders of the city. Throughout his career he gave the greatest encouragement

Portsmouth Police Fire Brigade's Model T Ford fire-engines on display in 1927.

Courtesy Mr. D.G. Dine

Portsmouth's long-serving Leyland-Metz turntable ladder seen here in 1933 with Supt. Charles Gould (right). *Courtesy James Cramer*

to the local volunteer brigades, particularly Fareham, which he visited often. In 1934 he became a member of the executive committee of the Royal Life Saving Society. His retirement as chief of the fire brigade came in 1937, and a year later he died.

Early in his career he led the brigade on some large fires. In May, 1920, F.J. Spillerware's household furnishers was burned down, and in February, 1922, the borough assisted when an armature shop in the Dockyard suffered a £4,500 fire. Biggest of this series of blazes was the £35,000 inferno that destroyed the Bayir Co. corset factory in January 1924. At this stage, the brigade's line-up of appliances had recently been augmented. In 1919, a new Dennis Gwynne 400-gallon-a-minute turbine pump was ordered for £870, followed by an

85-foot Merryweather motor-turntable-ladder and water tower in 1922.

Portsmouth's street alarm system, which was being introduced at about this time, showed again that everything except the lack of man-power was being catered for. After the first moves for a new street fire alarm system had been made in 1915, it came into operation in 1924. It was a Beasley-Gamewell combined fire and police telephonic and telegraphic closed circuit alarm, and 33 points were installed.

It was reckoned to be one of the finest systems in the country. So much so, that even the brigade's inner sanctum, former Chief Officer Pordage's office was converted to be the system's new battery room.

But nothing stopped the fires. In 1924, four-and-a-half tons of furniture stored in a steam wagon was burned out at a loss of £3,500. In May 1925, a Landport garage was burned down (£5,000), and in July 1926, the United Board Institute in Queen Street, Portsea, was destroyed at a loss of £20,000. 1926 saw the upraising of Portsmouth from borough to city status, but it didn't improve the brigade. With each new fire, under-manned because of the impossible restrictions of the system, the brigade struggled against the odds.

So imagine the reaction in 1927, when, unbelievably, Portsmouth councillor Mr. E. Hall used as his election platform, a campaign to reduce the police fire brigade. A national fire magazine leaped into the argument. The city had "one of the worst fire stations in the world, three motor pumps, three motor tenders, one motor-turntable-ladder, one rescue van and only 18 men, giving undesirable two-man crews. It needs to be increased and not cut," it said. Common sense prevailed. Councillor Hall polled the lowest count, was defeated, and vowed he would never seek re-election in Portsmouth again.

As it was, the brigade struggled against 174 fire calls that year. The following year it was the same bad news. The national magazine used Portsmouth as the worst example in the country, with its "police brigade being insufficient to man the machines" and with its "rapidly decaying fire station". How embarrassing! All this came in the year when Portsmouth hosted the Professional Fire Brigades Association annual congress with fire displays and demonstrations and with visiting fire officers from all over Britain.

And the fires kept burning. In October 1928, Wymering's race course grandstand was burned down, and in December, Halls Garage in Clarendon Place, Southsea went up with £3,000 added to the fire loss. Sadly, the Plaza Cinema at Bradford Junction, Southsea was badly damaged in March 1929 when a £4,000 fire wrecked the operating box. In December, H.T. Goddard's wholesale egg warehouse in Staunton Street was burned with a loss of £17,000

and in March 1931 a wholesale grocery store in Southsea was lost in a £3,000 blaze.

Everything the Corporation tried, short of actually tackling the man-power problem, only heaped criticism and ridicule on the city. It introduced one scheme in 1931 supposedly to augment the size of the brigade, which brought only national ridicule. The brilliant idea was to recruit four new young men, pay each one the "magnificent sum" of £2 a week, and then transfer them into the police force after three years as beat policemen. This, at a time when the city's population had increased to 250,000.

"This plan merely worsens the dark stain on the municipal escutcheon of the city of Portsmouth, where the Corporation is content to use its fire engines as ornaments," said the national fire magazine. Pretty strong words, but they needed saying. Traders were beginning to worry about attracting visitors to a resort becoming notorious for its "fire defencelessness".

Worse was to come. In 1934, a disastrous £250,000 fire destroyed the huge Co-operative departmental store and brought the wrath of local and national press down on the city's shoulders.

The brigade sent two station officers, eight firemen and three boys to this major outbreak. Young civilians grabbed the hoses, and only the arrival of the Royal Marine Dockyard Police Fire Brigade saved the remainder of the shops in Fratton Road, although nothing could save the Co-op.

Probably the most scathing criticism ever followed this debacle. "Virtually criminal under-manning of the city's fire brigade" produced the "lamentable display" of a brigade "totally incapable" of dealing with such fires. The fire spread resulted from "the insane desire of the Corporation to economize at the expense of the fire brigade. It is the city corporation that stands in the pillory," said the national comment.

Think of the only step the authorities could take to make matters worse – and they took it. They tried to counter the criticism by

Disastrous fire at the Co-op, Fratton Road, in 1934. Certainly one way of keeping cool! (See page 19).

Fire-fighting at the front of the Co-op.

Fire-fighting the Co-op blaze from the head of the turntable ladder.

All hands to the pumps at the rear of the Co-op.

arranging a test call – and it was a disaster. While all the fire engines were answering the test call at the mental hospital, a real call came in. Five policemen were eventually rounded up and with no fire engines left, they all bundled off to the scene in the only available vehicle – an ambulance! Even on the test call, which the brigade had arranged in advance, it took 25 minutes to get all the machines to the hospital, and the whole episode was headlined a "fiasco" in the national fire press.

During this period the expansion of the city boundaries to include Farlington resulted in the taking over of the one-man Farlington Parish Fire Brigade, complete with wooden hand-cart. Of greater use were the fire-engines which had been added to the brigade's stock during the final decade before its responsibilities ended. In 1925, a Leyland motor engine costing £1,235 was added, a Dennis rescue tender was purchased in 1931, and in 1936 a Dennis six-cylinder light motor pump with a 30-foot ladder and a Leyland six-cylinder 500-gallon-a-minute motor pump with a 35-foot ladder, completed the purchases.

The fires never stopped. In February 1935 an electricity sub-station suffered a £10,000 fire and within weeks a £9,000 blaze burned out the roof and upper floors of an experimental shop in H.M.S. Vernon.

A basic change in the organization of the fire service in Britain was fast approaching, and for Portsmouth it wasn't any too soon. On January 26, 1938 another fire brought a £20,000 loss. This time Wall and Attwool's electrical dealers in Crasswell Street, Landport went up, despite the efforts of five pumps and a turntable ladder.

In 1938 a new law was passed, fundamentally important in the history of the British fire service, as it placed an obligatory duty on local authorities to administer the fire service for the very first time. While it was in the process of being fully implemented, World War II intervened and emergency provisions to combat wartime conditions were introduced.

Saved! Portsmouth fire-fighters performing ladder rescues at the Fratton Park Tattoo before the war.   Courtesy The News

The few! Portsmouth's Police Fire Brigade members, led by their chief officer, Superintendent Charles Gould (centre front row) in 1936.

Left to right (back row) – Constable Ron Organ; Apprentice Fireman Albert Swan; Police Fireman Alf Wright; Police Fireman Harry Whiteman; Police Fireman Danny Kewell; Constable Sidney Boyland; Police Fireman George Watson; Police Fireman John L. Johnson; Police Fireman "Shep" Shepherd; Police Fireman Frederick Smith; Constable Sidney Groom; Apprentice Fireman Charles Daish. (front row) – Police Fireman George Longford; Police Fireman Bert Prior; Sergeant Harry Hicks; Sergeant William Hawkins; Supt. Charles Gould; Sergeant "Nick" Nicholas; Police Fireman "Chink" Colwell; Police Fireman Harry Colverson; Police Fireman Robert French.

Hence, the decade from 1938 to 1948 which embraces the war period was probably the most important in the evolution of the modern fire service, with Portsmouth seeing the changes typical of the whole country. In the city before that time there had existed the police and Dockyard brigades as we have seen, with auxiliary firemen undergoing training. A year later war broke out, the Auxiliary Fire Service began a new active fire-fighting role, and in 1941 all these fire-fighters came under the umbrella of the National Fire Service. Finally, in 1948 the responsibility for fire-fighting was handed back to the local authorities – the real birth of the modern fire service as we know it today.

Lost! Little remained inside the Airspeed factory, Airport Service Road, Hilsea after this fire shortly before the war. Courtesy G.E.B. Brunner

With the memory of the disastrous 1934 Co-op fire still in people's minds, the effect of the new combination of police brigade backed up by the new force, the Auxiliary Fire Service, was watched with keen interest. Portsmouth's auxiliary firemen staged a large-scale display of fire-fighting methods on Southsea Common on the evening of June 7, and about 2,000 spectators were given the opportunity of seeing these volunteers put through their paces.

A real test of the new combination came shortly before the war when, on April 27, 1939 J. Sherwell's engineers and founders caught fire in Unicorn Road. Before the flames were brought under control the building was burned out and two other stores damaged.

After the outbreak of war but before the first bombing raid on the city, the fire-fighting combination was faced with three more big

Portsmouth's Auxiliary Fire Service women adorn the Leyland Metz turntable ladder in 1937. Courtesy M. Russell

Light portable Beresford "Stork" trailer pumps on parade in Park Road for use by the Auxiliary Fire Service in 1938. Courtesy The News

Sergeant Harry Hicks in the police fire brigade multi-purpose van towing trailer pumps. Courtesy The News

War is coming. Men of the Auxiliary Fire Service and police fire brigade exercise water-relaying through the streets of Portsmouth.

Courtesy The News

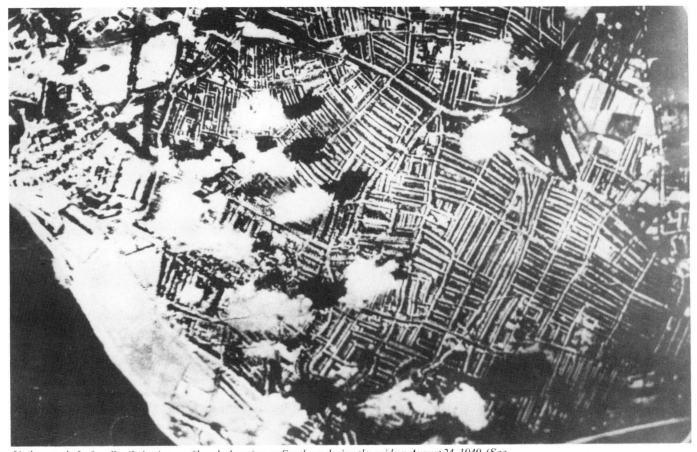

Under attack. Luftwaffe pilot's picture of bombs bursting on Southsea during the raid on August 24, 1940. (See page 27).

Courtesy G.E.B. Brunner

fires in a Southsea factory, a Copnor brickfield, and then a real inferno. On May 23, 1940 Woolworth's departmental store in Commercial Road caught fire. Four police pumps and the turntable ladder fought the fire with the massive assistance of 80 auxiliary firemen with eight Auxiliary Fire Service pumps. Woolworths was burned out with a loss of £182,000 and 250 people found themselves suddenly jobless.

But even this blaze was a mild prelude to the real brunt of the terrible ordeal that eventually rested on the shoulders of these fire-fighters. For the really disastrous fire-bomb raids on Portsmouth that would probably have laid waste the entire city but for the courageous work of the firemen and civil defence workers, came before the formation of the National Fire Service. In fact, it was because of the severity of the early raids like those on Portsmouth that the need for the National Fire Service was more clearly seen.

Portsmouth was only a few minutes flying distance from France and from its first raid on July 11, 1940 to the time when fire-fighting duties were transferred to the National Fire Service in August 1941, the city had 792 air-raid warnings – nearly two a day.

Of these raids, four were major attacks, leaving enormous fires blazing, and more than 50 others were fairly heavy raids. As early as August 1940, Portsmouth was suffering great damage. St. John's Church, Portsea was burned down on the 12th, when the Harbour Station also suffered a serious fire. Houses, shops, railways and the Dockyard were hit by 70 high-explosive bombs on August 24, when 125 people were killed, and on August 28, 30 private properties were destroyed by fire. A raid on October 7 left Pickford's Furniture Depository in Swan Street, and Government House both in ruins, and there were ten more raids during October and November, most of which started fires.

At this time, the position of Chief Constable and director of the fire brigade in Portsmouth – vacated by Mr. T. Davies – was filled by

Police Superintendent Arthur Charles West of the Hampshire Constabulary, who took over in the middle of the raids.

After the bombers had left on December 5 one serious fire, nine medium fires, and 20 small fires were blazing, and two of the city's hospitals had been hit. But these raids, bad as they were, gave no clue as to what was to befall the city on January 10, 1941. Portsmouth was attacked by 300 bombers in the most terrible fire-bomb raid it had ever experienced. They dropped 450 high-explosive bombs which effectively shattered most of the city's water mains. They then rained down 25,000 incendiary bombs to start massive fires which the firemen, without water, could not hope to contain. Within hours, 28 separate fires had each grown to "major" proportions. The city's splendid Guildhall was destroyed and the main shopping centres in Palmerston Road, Kings Road and Commercial Road were laid in ruins.

Six churches, the Eye and Ear Hospital, part of the Royal Portsmouth Hospital, Clarence Pier, the Hippodrome, three cinemas, the Dockyard school, the Connaught Drill Hall, Central Hotel, the Royal Sailors Rest, and the Salvation Army Citadel were all destroyed. That night there were 2,314 fires and 1,000 Auxiliary Fire Service men and pumps drafted into the city, together with the mobilization of the naval, Royal Marine, military and Home Guard personnel.

Afterwards, the Lord Mayor, Sir Dennis Daley paid tribute on behalf of the city to the fire-fighters who had worked "untiringly" in dangerous and difficult conditions. Several lost their lives that night among the final death toll of 171 for the raid.

Portsmouth learned quickly the awful lesson spelled out by that dreadful night. At the height of the fire-fighting, water was being relayed for more than three miles so a completely new emergency water supply system was needed.

A five-point plan was introduced in the city to counter the fracturing of water mains by bombing. These were the installation of emergency water dams – some steel and some brick – in various strategic positions; three concrete slipways to be built to Southsea foreshore; dry-risers to be installed in certain places; and the laying of four miles of six-inch steel piping, costing £5,600. Lastly they needed to find a more effective system of dealing with incendiary bombs – and quick.

Portsmouth's Emergency Committee was told that under the Fire Prevention (Business Premises) Order, the response from volunteers to undertake fire watching duties throughout the city was excellent, with 12,000 people having signed on. But this still did not cover all areas as naturally, people wanted to watch their own homes.

As a result, it was resolved that the principle of compulsory Civil Service Defence should be adopted. By mid-October, 28,250 men had been registered as fire guards. Their effectiveness became increasingly important as the year progressed, and the city came in for more massive air-raids.

In mid-March there were four heavy bombing raids, three of which were on successive nights beginning on March 9. The Dockyard, Portsea, Southsea and Fratton were badly hit and suffered widespread damage, and on March 10, thousands of incendiary bombs and 250 high-explosive bombs rained down on the city. Its hard-pressed fire-fighters were reinforced by 1,250 Auxiliary Fire Service personnel drafted in from outside, together with six mobile canteens.

Fire-fighting continued all night and day but on March 11 the bombers were back. This time they unloaded thousands of incendiaries on the north of the city – many falling on Portsdown Hill. The 20 high-explosive bombs which fell caused heavy casualties. There was a respite for two nights, but on March 14, when the Luftwaffe returned, four fire-watchers were among the city's dead. These March raids fractured 60 water mains, and parts of the city were without water for short periods.

April brought a new series of bad raids. Casualties were heavy –

In the blitz. Firemen trying to save part of Commercial Road early in 1941.

Courtesy The News

Bombed and burned out. McIlroys store was blitzed in Commercial Road in April 1941, and the great fires left empty shells in Chandos Street and round the Royal Sailors Rest.

Courtesy The News

Battered. Once Commercial Road's fires were out, life carried on in the rubble-strewn street.

Courtesy The News

with 110 people killed or injured in one raid on April 8 – but the fire-watching scheme was having its desired effect. After a seven-and-a-half hour raid on April 17, fire-watchers had done their work well, and only nine small fires were burning. The Auxiliary Fire Service soon dealt with them.

Portsmouth Police Fire Brigade's Senior Executive Officer (Superintendent Albert Edward Johnson) received a bravery award during the month for "coolness and courage" during the supervision of rescues during the raids, and Auxiliary Fireman N. Nabarro received the George Medal for his work fire-fighting and rescuing through the raids.

A particularly fierce raid on April 27 left up to two-thirds of the city damaged, and major fires were blazing in the Dockyard and around McIlroys store in Commercial Road when the bombers left. But the raids thinned out in May, and by June and July the Luftwaffe was hardly seen over Portsmouth.

By this time the nation had decided that to better protect itself from the bombing raids, the fire brigade needed to be nationalized, and on August 8, 1941 the National Fire Service came into being. In Portsmouth the Police Fire Brigade and the Auxiliary Fire Service were transferred accordingly to Government control. Between the outbreak of war and the formation of the National Fire Service the air-raid warning had sounded 792 times, and in the year of air attacks, 1,500 heavy bombs had been dropped. Of the city's 70,000 houses, 65,000 had suffered some kind of damage.

More work was being done to counter the problem of fractured water mains and one type of pre-cast concrete water-tank, designed and used in Portsmouth, was copied by other towns and cities. The brainchild of the city's Deputy City Engineer, Mr. W.E.C. Chamberlain, the tank held 3,500 gallons, and Portsmouth was building four a day. But the city entered 1942 receiving much less attention from the Luftwaffe than in the previous two years. Portsmouth's National Fire Service fire-fighters were tested in June 1942 when the Crown Bedding Company factory in Old Portsmouth was destroyed in a spectacular blaze which caused £80,000 worth of damage.

In 1942 Canadian fire-fighters forged strong links with the men serving in the National Fire Service, and some Canadians were drafted into the city to augment the National Fire Service in case enemy activity intensified. In fact, bombing raids were rare with only two in August and a heavier raid on December 16 when 20 houses were wrecked and 200 damaged.

At a fire in Campbells furniture store, Elm Grove, Southsea, which at one time threatened to engulf a whole block of premises, a new branch of the National Fire Service, the Salvage Squad came into operational duty. Their work in removing stock from the blazing store enabled fire-fighters equipped with breathing apparatus to get at the fire and confine it to the one store, thus saving the block.

Men of the Portsmouth Detachment of the Corps of Canadian Fire Fighters drafted into the city to augment the National Fire Service. (See page 30). *Courtesy G.E.B. Brunner*

Church parade in Portsmouth for the National Fire Service men of Fire Force 14 in 1942. *Courtesy The News*

National Fire Service competition drills in Portsmouth in 1943. Men of Fire Force 14 in action.   Courtesy G.E.B. Brunner

For the fire-fighters, 1943 was a quiet year, sandwiched between the dreadful years of the bombing raids and before the enormous build-up of fire cover which became necessary for the preparations to D-Day and the Normandy landings.

In 1943 Mr. John Leslie Johnson became Assistant Commander of the Portsmouth Fire Force under Commander S. H. Charters, who commanded the region. One of the very few serious bombing raids on August 15 started 50 fires, with a boathouse and timber store at Langstone among the targets set on fire. In fact, this raid was linked very closely to the massive preparations for D-Day. The allies had launched a full-scale exercise towards occupied France, called "Harlequin". A force grouped, embarked from the south coast ports, and sailed to within a few miles of the occupied French coast – drawing this bombing raid against Portsmouth as a reprisal.

When the mighty allied invasion army was concentrated on the south coast in preparation for D-Day in June 1944, the Portsmouth area was reckoned to be one of the greatest single fire hazards anywhere in the world. Concealed in woodlands and under camouflage for miles around were huge dumps of oil, petrol, ammunition and stores. Any large scale devastation by fire could have crippled Operation Overlord – the invasion itself.

So nine months before D-Day, the National Fire Service started to make massive preparations in close liaison with the fighting services and the civil defence authorities. It was plain that the National Fire Service would have to protect not only the volatile dumps but also the points of embarkation – and, not least, the vast invasion fleet when it assembled in Spithead and the Solent.

To meet this risk, many Royal Naval Auxiliary craft were converted into fire boats, and volunteer National Fire Service men went into training at the fireboat school established at Mobey House, Gosport. These volunteers were eventually provided with a uniform consisting of cap, reefer jacket, oilskin coat, sou'wester and rubber boots.

Preparations also involved a major building programme. This provided for new annexes at the Fire Force Headquarters, two reinforcement bases, five new fire-stations, and the conversion of another eight stations for use on a whole-time instead of a part-time basis. A stock of 40 tons of food was distributed to various stores, and three weeks supplies of rations were sent to the men in the Isle of Wight in case the island should be cut off from communications with the mainland. The National Fire Service also set up a vast telephone and radio network embracing Hampshire, West Sussex and the Isle of Wight. Static water supplies also had to be provided for the many isolated camps and depots.

Early in 1944 there was an invasion of another kind as hundreds of National Fire Service men and women were drafted in from the Midlands and the north to reinforce the personnel in this area.

Shortly afterwards there was a call for volunteers for the National Fire Service Overseas Contingent for duty "if and when required" with the fighting services when they were established on the other side of the Channel.

As D-Day approached the National Fire Service men, living in camps with the troops, became subject to ever-tightening military restrictions. First, two-day leave was stopped, then annual leave went the same way. Later a ban was imposed on travel outside a 25-mile limit – and finally the troops and firemen were sealed off from the outside world.

As the great invasion fleet assembled at Spithead and in the Solent the fireboats began their brief but invaluable commission. Controlled by the Admiralty at Fareham, these craft included the ex-Icelandic trawlers Channel Fire and Ocean Fire, and the former luxury yachts Lowayo and Laureate. In the crowded anchorage, mishaps were inevitable, and the fireboat crews found themselves spending as much time pumping water out of holed vessels as

Ill-fated National Fire Service fireboat Kittihawke II, which was sunk in a Portsmouth Harbour collision. (See page 33). Courtesy G.E.B. Brunner

National Fire Service sea-going fireboat Laureate, based in Portsmouth Harbour. Courtesy G.E.B. Brunner

Former luxury motor-yacht Lowayo, now a National Fire Service fireboat in 1944 based in Portsmouth. Courtesy G.E.B. Brunner

pumping water to quench fires.

Between May and the end of August the fireboats in the waters of Portsmouth Command attended 89 special service calls exclusive of fire calls. On the first day of invasion operations, fireboat NAB 503 gained almost a "battle honour" after being sent to help a landing barge laden with 10,000 gallons of oil, which had been holed on a submerged object at the entrance to Langstone Harbour. This was one of the key D-Day bases and the stricken barge was in danger of sinking and blocking the fairway. After three hours the National Fire Service crew had pumped the oil and water out of the barge, and it was safely beached.

The same fireboat went to the rescue when another barge started to founder off an embarkation beach and threatened to obstruct operations.

On May 4, fireboat Laureate travelled 23 miles out to sea to fight a blaze in a motor-torpedo-boat which had been hit by the enemy, but crewmen on fireboat NAB 518 couldn't believe their ears when they were sent the other way – to stand by a hay rick fire on the shore of the estuary. Make no mistake, it was an urgent call because the landing barges loaded with petrol and ammunition were moored near the blazing hay.

On April 11, the fleet suffered the loss of the fireboat Kittihawke II, involved in a collision with an Admiralty tug in Portsmouth Harbour. She sank in three minutes. The firemen were picked up but when the Kittihawke was later raised she was found to be a write-off.

The National Fire Service was also busy ashore – particularly on May 30 when a big blaze set ammunition flying at Park Gate near Fareham. Two Sherman tanks were burned out but the firemen managed to save four self-propelling guns and a jeep. Bullets were flying round the men as they fought the blaze, and for good measure they were warned that the ammunition inside the vehicles included a few mines.

At the peak of the invasion embarkations, the National Fire

Protecting the D-Day invasion forces from fire fell to Portsmouth's National Fire Service men. They dealt with these two tank fires in 1944.

Courtesy G.E.B. Brunner

Service in the Portsmouth area was manning 614 appliances of various types and many ingenious measures were taken to ensure a continuous supply of water in the event of heavy bombing putting mains out of commission. But the Luftwaffe was in no position to retaliate in strength – and so the great fleet sailed, majestic and unstoppable to liberate Europe.

The National Fire Service record for that day reads, "The fireboat crews watched their charges leave for France with a sense of frustration that they could not accompany them. Their duties were not over, however, as ships crippled by enemy action and in danger of sinking were met by fireboats as they limped home, and saved by the fireboats pumps." Finally, on September 26, 1944 the Fireboat

The City's thanks to the departing Canadian fire-fighters expressed by Fire Force Commander S.H. Charters at the Royal Beach Hotel. (See page 36).
Courtesy G.E.B. Brunner

Service was accorded its own "naval review" in Osborne Bay with an inspection by Admiral Sir Charles Little.

While the invasion of France was in full swing the menace of the V.1. Doodlebug – Hitler's new terror weapon – was unleashed on the south coast. For several anxious months before the V.1. sites could be overrun, the flying bombs crossed the Channel. On June 25 one hit Locksway Road, Milton, with heavy casualties and damage, and at least nine others crashed into the sea around Portsmouth and south-east Hampshire. Later in June and July Portsmouth's fire-fighters were relieved to watch the Doodlebugs flying over the city on their journey northwards to London.

As the fortunes of war improved on the Continent the fire readiness back in England was allowed to be relaxed. On October

In its heyday the National Fire Service Band of Fire Force 14 strikes up a pose in 1944. (See page 41).
Courtesy G.E.B. Brunner

Fletchers Corset factory just before Christmas, 1960. (See page 39).

22, 1944 fire-guard duties in Portsmouth were suspended and 32,000 fire-watchers were released. On November 15-16 the Overseas Contingent was disbanded, and towards December the Canadian fire-fighters were allowed to return home – after enjoying an honorary luncheon on December 6 at the Royal Beach Hotel.

At the end of 1944 statisticians translated the entire war, all the bombings, deaths, injuries, fires and horrors into a telling set of figures. Portsmouth had endured 67 raids, 930 people had been killed, 2,837 injured, 6,625 homes were destroyed, and 75,435 houses damaged. As Portsmouth only had 70,000 houses the figures clearly showed that some houses had been bombed repeatedly. The war had given the city its worst ever fire-blitzes. The Auxiliary Fire Service had borne the brunt in the worst years, while the National Fire Service did its greatest work in providing fire protection in the preparations for the Normandy invasions. When the war came to an end the National Fire Service remained, and one of its first jobs in Southsea was to build a new fire station in Somers Road.

About 120,000 bricks, saved from bomb sites in Portsmouth, were used in its construction. They were recovered, cleaned and laid by the National Fire Service firemen who also did the joinery work, plumbing and electrical fittings. Designed, planned and built by the personnel, the station was officially opened on January 11, 1946 when the Lord Mayor called out the brigade by pulling down a switch outside the station. This set the bells in the building ringing and the £7,000 station was open.

Late in 1946, the National Fire Service together with the Dockyard Fire Brigade fought a serious explosion and fire which killed two men and injured 13 on the Maxwell Brander, a ship undergoing refit in the Dockyard on November 29. Two Portsmouth firemen received awards in recognition of courage and devotion shown during the fire. Fireman Joseph Dunaway, serving at Craneswater Park station, received the British Empire Medal, and Leading Fireman Ernest Penwarden, serving at Somers Road station,

You don't get too many farm fires in Portsmouth, but they've had their moments. Bonfire night, 1969, brought out half the city brigade to a "ten-pumper" at Southwick. Courtesy The News

Crouching on a dung-heap, this city fireman gets to grips with a Portsdown Hill humdinger of a farm rubbish fire. Courtesy The News

received the King's Commendation. While "working in intense heat they succeeded in bringing out the two ship's crewmen who subsequently died."

Mr. John Leslie Johnson of Portsmouth, Assistant Fire Force Commander of No. 14 Fire Force was appointed Chief Fire Officer of Portsmouth with effect from April 1, 1948 and that year the National Fire Service was disbanded and fire-fighting responsibilities returned to the local authorities.

Thus, Portsmouth City Fire Brigade came into being on April 1, 1948 with the implementation of the Fire Services Act of the previous year. It ceased to exist on April 1, 1974 exactly 26 years later when it became part of the newly constituted Hampshire Fire Brigade with which it was amalgamated. During those 26 years it was described as a "compact brigade with an immense responsibility", operating at all times with just six pumping machines and three special appliances from its three operational stations.

With this force it provided fire-cover for Portsmouth Naval Base, including the navy's warships, and ever-increasing volume of light industry, a busy commercial centre, the city's increasing quantity of office block accommodation, the large hotel and guest-house industry at Southsea, and a growing commercial dockland. Within the brigade's 14 square mile patch the population of the city has been classified as the second most dense in the country, and in 26 years the brigade answered more than 38,000 fire calls. The primary function of any brigade is to save life, and the fact that only 49 people died in fires in Portsmouth during the brigade's span is a tribute to the way it protected the population of around 200,000 people.

For the brigade's first six years there were no fatalities in Portsmouth from fire, and 50 per cent of all its fatal fires occurred in the five year spell from 1963 to 1967. Worst year of all was 1963 when seven people died, and the majority of victims were elderly folk who died in fires in their homes.

There were only 13 really major blazes in the city in those 26 years, five being in factories, two on board warships in the Naval Base, two in the Dockyard itself, two in the commercial shopping trade, one in an oil tanker at sea, and one in a theatre. No brigade personnel was ever killed on a fire.

The brigade only had two chief officers, Mr. Johnson who commanded it for the first 14 years, and Mr. George Brunner who was in charge for the latter 12 years. After occupying four fire stations on its formation, the brigade made history by being the first in the country to complete its post-war building programme with the opening of the new Copnor Road headquarters in 1957, from which time the Brigade operated from three stations.

One of these – the station built by the National Fire Service firemen at Southsea – remained in existence throughout the 26 years of the brigade.

On its formation the brigade's establishment was 137 personnel – 131 uniformed members, one uniformed fire prevention officer and five non-uniformed personnel – all under the command of Chief Fire Officer Johnson. Net cost of the brigade in the first financial year was £58,990 or 0.47 per cent of the city council's budget, a percentage which remained fairly constant, being set at 0.49 per cent (£238,405) in the 1968/69 budget, for example.

A 60-hour week was operated originally, with two watches working a five-day week followed by a five-night week. Its four original stations were at Somers Road, Southsea; Hilsea Fire Station (a requisitioned garage) in London Road; Cosham Fire Station (the requisitioned Waverley Cinema) in High Street; and the administrative headquarters building at 44, Craneswater Park, Southsea (a requisitioned house formerly used by the Auxiliary Fire Service).

From these stations it was considered that the statutory obligations of fire cover for the city in 1948 could be provided. This meant that two fire engines had to arrive at any fire within five minutes of the call, with supporting pumps arriving inside 20 minutes. At all times fire cover was maintained with two pumping appliances at each of the three operational stations, plus two turntable ladders, one of which was on the run at all times, and with an emergency tender and a salvage tender completing the list of front-line machines.

There were 4,883 hydrants in the city in 1948 when it was also served by 59 police/fire street alarms which remained in operation until 1955, when they were discontinued.

When recruiting for the Auxiliary Fire Service was recommenced, enormous recruiting problems plagued the city. The aim was to have 254 auxiliary firemen and 25 women in Portsmouth, yet enrolment produced just 18 men and 15 women, and despite constant efforts towards recruitment it had only risen to 51 men and 24 women by 1950.

Within 48 hours of its formation the brigade tackled its first big fire when Sydenham's Timber Yard at Rudmore went up, and it was faced with an even sterner test on March 21, 1949 when fire broke out in an all wooden warehouse in the Dockyard. Eleven pumps from the Dockyard brigade, the city brigade, and Hampshire Fire Service fought this one before it was under control.

With new buildings and fire engines, the brigade enjoyed a steady march of progress in the early 1950's. When the Lord Mayor (Alderman Albert Johnson) opened the new Cosham Fire Station on January 1, 1952 history was made, it being the first permanent station to be completed in the city.

Two years later the Secretary of State authorized the beginning of a new headquarters building at Copnor to replace the Hilsea and Craneswater Park buildings. A replacement programme of the brigade's fire engines also began in 1952, and by 1957, when Hilsea's pump was replaced, all the wartime or pre-war pumping appliances had been renewed.

In contrast to this progress, the Auxiliary Fire Service continued to labour under difficult recruiting problems for its very existence.

House-to-house canvassing in 1952 and 1953 raised the women's figures to 36, and dragged the men's total up to 91 – a sad figure that was still less than 40 per cent of the target. This slumped in the next three years to 60 men.

After six years with no loss of life in the city from fire, the early months of 1954 – a period of severe and harsh cold – brought a dramatic change. Five elderly people died in five fires attended by the brigade. Two years later, on December 27, 1956, came the only multiple fatality from fire in the brigade's history when two people died in a house in Lennox Road, Southsea, in a Christmas tragedy. Earlier the same year, on February 10, the brigade experienced its second major blaze, again in the Dockyard, when a 200-year-old timber store was reduced to charred ruins.

Copnor Road fire headquarters were opened in April 29, 1957, and with it, the city became the first county borough in England to complete its building programme for the fire service. It meant the end of the Hilsea Fire Station and the Craneswater Park premises, and was accompanied by the first increase in the brigade's personnel. There was no such luck for the Auxiliary Fire Service. The continuing saga of recruiting woe spread to the women and in 1959 the women's total slipped to just 14, and never again recovered.

That same year was one of the most significant in the development of fire prevention in Portsmouth. There was one officer in 1948, but eventually the brigade's fire prevention efforts grew into a complete department led by a divisional officer. In 1959 the first of a series of acts of legislation was introduced which drastically increased the department's number of visits and work load. In one year the Portsmouth Corporation Act 1959 called for 844 visits by fire prevention officers, and greatly increased the department's responsibilities.

Managements of the city's largest department stores were requesting that fire prevention officers visit them following national and international fire disasters in department stores soon after the war, for example.

In 1960, for the first time in 12 years, the brigade faced a really major fire outside the Dockyard when Fletchers corset factory blazed in Regent Street, Mile End on December 15, causing damaged estimated at £250,000. It is said that blazing corsets were blasted out through the roof and floated down around amazed spectators at the height of the fire. It was the first of eight of the city's major fires to occur during Christmas holidays which gave birth to a "Christmas fire jinx" legend.

First important change for the brigade as it moved into the 1960's was the retirement of Chief Fire Officer Johnson and the appointment of Chief Fire Officer George Brunner, both men having served their early careers in the Portsmouth Police Fire Brigade before World War II.

Mr. Johnson joined the Portsmouth City Police Force in 1931 and transferred to its fire brigade section four years later. By 1940 he had been promoted to sergeant and when the National Fire Service was formed a year later he was appointed deputy to the Fire Force Commander of Area 14, covering Portsmouth, Eastern Hampshire and the Isle of Wight. Having been selected as Portsmouth's chief fire officer in September 1947 his first major responsibility was to organize the city brigade.

In 1952 he was awarded the King's Police and Fire Service Medal and his close connections with the St John Ambulance Association meant the brigade maintained a very high standard of first aid skill.

Mr. Brunner who replaced him joined the Portsmouth Police Fire Brigade in 1934 as an apprentice. He was one of those three boys sent to the disastrous fire which burned down the Co-op building in 1934 – that awesome blaze being the first that he ever attended. Throughout the war years he served with the National Fire Service in Portsmouth and the Isle of Wight, and in 1944 he was seconded to

Hilsea's corrugated iron church was well alight when the pump escape arrived.

Very little was saved.

First, get to your fire. Up the escape ladders in Fratton Road...

or hijack a boatman in the Camber Dock.

the Ministry of War Transport as Fire Officer to Port Said, Egypt.

Two years later he returned as officer-in-charge of Hilsea Fire Station, and on the formation of the city fire brigade he was made station officer. After a temporary appointment as a fire service college instructor he moved into Hampshire Fire Service in 1957 and when he later became Nottinghamshire Fire Service's senior staff officer, he served under Chief Fire Officer J.B. Vickery – who had also been one of Portsmouth's pre-war firemen.

In 1961 a move to Wiltshire Fire Brigade preceded his taking the Portsmouth chief fire officer's appointment the following year.

1963 was the beginning of the worst five years the city ever experienced for fatal fires since World War II. The severe winter of '63 brought seven deaths in seven fires, and by the end of 1967, 24 people had died in five years. In 1965 the "Christmas Jinx" struck again when a very smoky fire caused £327,000 worth of damage at the Landport Drapery Bazaar department store on that fateful date, December 22.

In the same year, a prophetic warning about the future of the Auxiliary Fire Service was sounded, when, in his annual report, Mr. Brunner recorded, "Further development of this important civil defence service is likely to be seriously hindered if not prevented altogether by the lack of suitable accommodation and facilities."

For the first time a link was forged between the brigade and the Duisburg Fire Brigade as part of the city's civic twinning programme. Duisburg's chief fire officer, Herr Richard Frosch visited Portsmouth returning a visit made by Mr. Brunner to the German city the previous year. While the brigade opened one door there, another closed, for in 1965 the Portsmouth City Fire Brigade Band became the Portsmouth City Band, and all connections with the brigade were severed. Originally the band which had its ancestry with the No. 14 Area National Fire Service Band, had close ties with the brigade, but for many years prior to 1965 there was not a fireman left blowing a horn or even tinkling a cymbal.

When the "Christmas Jinx" struck again in 1967 it produced probably one of the biggest fires ever tackled by the city brigade. On Christmas Eve it was called to John Palmers brush factory an extensive building packed with highly flammable goods, all of which went up in flames. The entire brigade plus nearly a dozen more machines from Hampshire Fire Service fought to prevent the fire engulfing surrounding properties and damage was later put at £250,000. At this time in late 1967 the brigade received its own radio scheme instead of having to rely on the joint police and fire brigade radio system.

Two fire-fighting forces ceased in Portsmouth in 1968 when both the Auxiliary Fire Service and the Portsmouth Dockyard Fire Brigade were disbanded as part of Government policy. The city brigade had always attended fires in the Dockyard to boost the establishment's own brigade, but after 1968 the sole responsibility for the naval base fell upon the brigade.

Fighting fires in the Dockyard means tackling blazes on warships. The development of breathing apparatus made the greatest single impact on the ability of firemen to get into ships and put out fires – but it is punishing work. Any fireman will testify that working blindly downwards through narrow hatches into ever-increasing heat to locate and knock out a fire in the bowels of a ship is his most feared nightmare. It is only in port brigades that this task is regularly encountered – and only in a naval port that the risk is multiplied by the inherent dangers of a warship.

During the brigade's 26 years there were more than 500 fires on warships in Portsmouth Dockyard. Worst year of all was in 1967 when firemen faced the danger on average once a week in dealing with 55 warship fires.

On most occasions the ship's crew dealt with the fire even before firemen arrived, but there were exceptions. Two of the most serious warship fires at Portsmouth in modern times were the fires on the aircraft carrier H.M.S. Victorious on November 11, 1967 and on the helicopter cruiser H.M.S. Blake on January 21, 1969.

Fighting factory fires. A plastics factory. Burrfields Road. Copnor in 1971 suffered a £20,000 loss...

...and a Farlington warehouse lost most of its roof.

Courtesy The News

Everything that haunts a fire-fighter about modern warship fires was present on the Victorious. Dense smoke filled compartments away from the fire, hiding it at first, the heat was intense, and worst of all, a sailor was lost in the heart of it all. Only courageous work by firemen working alongside the ship's crew contained the fire, but the sailor perished.

A far worse potential disaster faced the brigade and the Dockyard when a serious fire took hold of H.M.S. Blake when she was undergoing a refit in dry dock. Once again, smoke spread through the ship blocking the way for firemen and cutting off the escape route of 18 men trapped inside her and under the fire. Fate had left an unusual escape-hatch for them – a fitting in the ship's bottom which could be removed. The men dropped down into the dry dock and no-one was lost.

As for the Auxiliary Fire Service, it had enjoyed a slight flourish in its latter years, expanding in 1966 to a force of 119, its highest ever, but on March 28, 1968, Mr. Brunner's prophetic warning was realized. It had a final strength of 115 men and women when it took part in its last "stand-down" parade in the Guildhall Square and was disbanded. At this time the Auxiliary Fire Service in Portsmouth had £50,000 worth of equipment, its stock of vehicles including four self-propelled pumps, three special appliances, ten portable pumps, two motor-cycles, a command vehicle, and portable wireless equipment.

In the same year, local authority spending cuts temporarily stopped recruiting for the city brigade which had a bearing on its strength a year later.

But 1968 was remembered by the brigade for its last week, which together with the first week of the new year, brought fires the men will never forget. The "Christmas Jinx" raised its head not once but three times so that in less than a fortnight between December 29 and January 9, the brigade tackled three major fires in factories not a mile apart, which caused the colossal loss of more than £2,250,000.

Under the foam and inside the wetsuits — they are all firemen. The "foamies" were exercising in high-expansion foam.

The Brigade's Sub-Aqua Club, which did pioneering work on the Mary Rose.

Courtesy The News

On December 29, Drings printing factory was badly damaged at Hilsea in a fire which brought the whole brigade into action, and which caused £186,000 worth of damage. Worse was to follows.

On January 7, 1969 the Metal Box factory, another huge building packed with highly flammable plastics suffered a fire which drew the whole brigade into action together with six Hampshire crews, which left half the building in ruins, and which caused damage amounting to £500,000. Within 48 hours fire crews could hardly believe their ears when the brigade was called to the same factory again. This time the other half, which they had fought so stubbornly

Chief Fire Officer George Brunner with the ladies of the city's new control room. (See page 45).
Left to right – Firewoman Sheila King (seated); Leading Firewoman Irene Cox; Senior Leading Firewoman Phyl MacGregor; Leading Firewoman May Barber; Leading Firewoman Dorothy Evans.

to save, was in flames. Once again the whole brigade was mobilized with six Hampshire crews, and damage totalled £1,600,000. A man was later acquitted of arson charges in court in connection with these two fires.

Continual increases in the brigade's fire prevention work load coincided with a considerable worsening of the brigade's manpower position in 1969. This was a legacy of the recruiting cut-back ordered the previous year, and left the brigade 16 men under strength.

In 1961 the Licencing Act almost doubled the number of fire prevention visits to 1,632 and the 1963 figure of 2,415 visits was more than all visits made by the brigade in the first eight years. A national fire prevention campaign was launched in 1965 when, in addition to the fire prevention department's 3,168 visits that year, operational crews made a further 2,342 house-to-house visits supporting the campaign. The weight of work continued to increase and although visits topped 3,750 in 1966, and 3,550 in 1969, Mr. Brunner's report for that year showed a back-log of work was still piling up.

In the early 1970's the brigade launched a new vehicle replacement programme amid grumblings in the city about the age and condition of the brigade's engines, some of which were nearly 20 years old. Portsmouth's turntable ladders, for example, had a chequered history. The 1942 former National Fire Service turntable ladder remained in service all the 26 years of the brigade, either "on the run" or as the brigade spare. One Portsmouth museum curator saw it and wanted it as a centre-piece for a museum display, only to hear in astonishment that it was still in use! Portsmouth's other original turntable ladder, the Leyland-Metz 1933 machine was replaced by a Dennis-Metz in 1962. This appliance was dogged by mechanical failures and in 1967 when both turntable ladders were suffering defects, Eastbourne loaned the city a spare ladder.

Major changes within the brigade included plans for the increase in strength from 144 operational men riding machines to 165, and an overall increase from 184 personnel to 221, the extra manpower to be recruited by March 1975. The Dockyard and the commercial heart of the city nearby – including the Commercial Road, Arundel Street, civic centre and Polytechnic areas – were re-assigned as "A" risk areas – the highest priority – which meant the brigade had to get its first two fire engines to any fire there inside five minutes, with the third pump arriving in a further three minutes.

Another change meant that the city's station officers no longer rode to fires on the engines with the men as they had done since 1948. Instead they attended fires in private cars, making for "more effective use of their time".

In 1970 the brigade's new control room, with its new mobilizing system was introduced, making it one of the most modern in southern England at the time. Basically, before 1970, the men were alerted on the station by "putting down the bells" and the fire address was handed to them on a piece of paper. The new system meant alerting the men by a "warbler" sound throughout the station, followed by the address over a loud-speaker. In this way each man

What all firemen hate. A fire-call to a warship. Here, a city pump escape is control point at H.M.S. Blake in the Naval Base.

Courtesy The News

Warship fires are the worst. Breathing apparatus sets change, but the men are the same. Old-fashioned "proto" sets on H.M.S. Pellew, and new compressed air sets on H.M.S. Blake.

Courtesy The News

Portsmouth's third officer, Divisional Officer Jim Flynn (white helmet) at his famous exercise which was very spectacular.

Courtesy The News

Some exercise! Even suitably protected from flying slates, the author found it safer behind a nearby pump. *Courtesy The News*

knew where the fire was before his machine moved. Two or more stations could be alerted simultaneously, and the turn-out time was cut to less than 30 seconds.

In 1971 the first of the new fleet of five pumps came on the run, the Southsea pump having been replaced in 1967, and by 1974 the brigade had completed renewing all the city's fire engines.

Teaching architects fire-safety produced an amazing fire in 1970. The brigade took architect students, put them upstairs in a derelict building at Hilsea Barracks – and set fire to the ground floor beneath them! It had the desired effect. By the time they escaped, singed round the edges, each of them vowed to build fire-escapes first and then add the buildings on second.

It also had an undesired effect! The blaze got completely out of hand, swept through the building, blew through the roof, the smoke

A daunting blaze on the oil tanker Pacific Glory. But Portsmouth men together with crews from three more brigades beat it (See page 48).

Courtesy The News

closed Copnor Road, the brigade ended up with a "six-pump" fire, and the officer-in-charge, Jim Flynn became my new hero. "Flynn's folly" was a memorable success.

The 1970's opened with the longest and most arduous ship fire ever tackled by the brigade at sea when, on October 23, 1970 the Pacific Glory, a 77,000 ton tanker blew up and caught fire, killing 13 crewmen after a collision in the English Channel off the Isle of Wight.

Portsmouth men were out at sea together with fire-fighters from Hampshire, the Isle of Wight and Southampton for 44 hours tackling the terrifying inferno. Huge fireballs blew out of the ship, and the very sea around her was on fire with blazing oil. Several times the fire-fighters gained the upper hand, but new eruptions of fire wiped out their hard-won successes. Then, with a gale whipping up huge seas, the inferno grew again with its full ferocity, and all men were withdrawn. One man had his eyeballs seared by the heat, but next day, his colleagues started again.

A huge operation, codenamed "Solfire" was backing them. Foam was shipped out, the navy was there, tugs belted the tanker's superstructure with streaming water cannons, but in the end, it was the men who went aboard and fought the flames hand-to-hand down in the guts of the tanker who put the fire out.

Next day, I went afloat and alongside the hulk in Sandown Bay where it was still being battered by huge seas. Her blackened twisted decks were still strewn with the hoselines where the men had fought the fire. Great seas washed across her waist where she sat aground by the stern. It came as no surprise that three men of the Portsmouth brigade won British Empire Medals as a result of the operation.

This was the fourth major ship fire which the city brigade had tackled afloat in the Solent and at Spithead since 1965. The first was on February 12, 1965 when the City of Waterford, seriously involved in fire, was brought into the Solent and where the brigade won the battle after two days fire-fighting. It repeated the task when the MV

Hundreds of people owe their lives to the specialist skill of firemen at road crashes. Here, on Portsbridge they worked with ambulancemen and police to save this driver. Courtesy The News

48

Saving life at road crashes.. in a bus crash in Copnor Road, Copnor...

in a car crash on the Eastern Road...

Courtesy The News

in a crane crash off the Havant by-pass...

Courtesy The News

in a lorry crash at Southwick Hill Road, Cosham...

El Hassanni was brought to Spithead belching smoke and flame on November 4, 1967, and again for the MV Saale.

One of the city's most spectacular fires in 1971 turned Benney's derelict toy warehouse, a former church, into a blazing beacon at Rudmore. I was there early on when the first men went in through thickening smoke. Soon you could hear the shrill whistles blowing – the brigade's panic signal to get out quick. As the last man scuttled out, flames appeared at the windows.

Then an almighty fire-ball blew through the old church and columns of curling flame barrelled out of the windows, blasting shattered masonry across the road.

Three streets away a motorist heard the blaze, saw the fireball, was distracted, and drove straight into an oncoming car. Razor sharp slates came sliding down from the roof as it disintegrated putting several firemen in hospital, and the blaze wasn't held until the old church was a tottering shell.

It was one of a long series of bad fires in the derelict buildings dotted around the city, and, being unsafe, the city engineer ordered it to be knocked down. It was a rueful chief fire officer who commented later, "my blokes save 'em, and his blokes knock 'em down".

That year the city once again experienced the "Christmas Jinx" when early in December, soon after the arrival of Christmas stock, 13 units of the Tricorn shopping complex in Market Way, Landport, were damaged in a punishing fire. The whole brigade, together with Hampshire appliances were summoned, and damage was later put at £382,000. Technical problems in fighting such fires in multi-storey pre-cast concrete shopping complexes were so new that the fire attracted the interest of fire officers and engineers from throughout Britain.

And one problem defeated all their training manuals. Firemen were confronted with an excited monkey, lively llamas, and a loud-roaring lion loping around in the smoke as the fire disturbed a circus housed in the complex. The men knew what steps to take... great big ones in the opposite direction.

Bad hotel fires all over England prompted new fire regulations and brought about further enormous increases in the work load of the fire prevention department in 1972 with new requirements for immediate inspections of hotels, of which Southsea is packed.

On October 23, 1972 came the last major blaze tackled by the city brigade when boys playing with fireworks set fire to the Theatre Royal in Commercial Road. It had lain empty for years and a controversy was raging over its future. Soon after the brigade's arrival you could forget controversy. Now fire was raging over half the building, with the rear section well alight. A large operation using 12 pumps – the entire city brigade plus nearly 40 Hampshire men – was needed to contain the fire.

I covered it for The News, watching the roof first pour smoke, then disintegrate with cracking, banging tiles exploding as flames devoured it, licking skywards, seeming to engulf the fireman above on the turntable ladder. Half the building – including the architecturally much-admired auditorium – was saved, and the threat to the remainder of Commercial Road, at risk at the height of the blaze, was averted.

Then the "Christmas Jinx" struck for the eighth and final time in another expensive fire. This time the brigade sent five pumps and the turntable ladder to the English Abrasives factory on the Fratton Industrial Estate, where giant industrial ovens worth £100,000 were ruined in the blaze on December 15, 1972.

All Portsmouth held its breath next when the unthinkable happened. On February 26, 1973, H.M.S. Victory caught fire. Smoke filled one deck, 100 visitors were ushered off, but the firemen couldn't reach the flames. Sparked by a blowlamp, they were spreading between the two layers of hull planking.

Ladders bridged the gap between dockside and hull, shipwrights were called in, holes cut in the hull, and only after several anxious hours were they sure the hoses inside the timbers had quelled the flames. H.M.S. Victory was saved, but ever since blowlamps have

Take any emergency other than fire — and you'll find the fireman there, too. They were there, making safe this crane in Portsmouth Dockyard.

Courtesy The News

*Navy fire-fighters hit an oil blaze in Portsmouth Dockyard with foam.
Every city fireman was called in for this inferno in 1970.* Courtesy Royal Navy

*Insurance companies sort out other people's
fires. Here's a fire at insurance offices in the
Guildhall Square for a change in 1971.* Courtesy The News

Two-in-a-month. September 1971 saw a spectacular night fire in an Old Polytechnic building in Lion Terrace...

and a daytime inferno when a contractor's demolition fire took off at the Duchess of Kent Barracks, Southsea.

Inside the fire-ravaged Polytechnic Building, Lion Terrace. Damage amounted to some £32,000.

Living up ladders! This fireball nearly took the sub-officer off this ladder at the Pack Club at Eastney...

and off ladders, balancing on narrow ledges at the Co-op warehouse blaze in North End...

Courtesy The News

been banned.

With only three months remaining before the brigade ceased to be, the headquarters building was the scene of an unveiling ceremony. On February 18, 1974 the Lord Mayor, Coun. J.P.N. Brogden unveiled a plaque commemorating the opening of a new extension. During 1973 and early 1974 a £60,000 modernization and extension programme had been completed on the building, adding a new floor above the appliance room.

While the work was in progress the city was served by a temporary "action post" in Stubbington Avenue, North End, which accommodated one pump and its crew for nine months, during which time this machine answered more than 1,000 fire calls.

The only disappointment for the brigade with its fire stations was that despite attempts dating from the late 1950's, a replacement station was never built in Southsea during the brigade's era to replace the "temporary" building in Somers Road constructed from the bomb-site bricks. On many occasions projects for a new station were shelved for financial reasons, and in later years, difficulties of access to planned major road developments in the area around the station caused further delays.

However, in February 1974 the City Council took the final decision to promote a compulsory purchase order to obtain the additional land to replace the station on the existing site – and the new station was opened eventually on November 7, 1978, four years after the city brigade had gone.

Although the city brigade ceased to exist on April 1, 1974, the stages of amalgamation with Hampshire began on February 25 when mobilization of the city's fire-engines was transferred to the Winchester headquarters of the county brigade. And then came that last notable fire dealt with by the city brigade just four days before April 1 when five pumps were needed to quell the flames in the Eye and Ear Hospital, Grove Road North, Southsea.

Chief Fire Officer Brunner, who had recieved the Queen's Fire

"An almighty fire-ball blew through the old church"... (See page 50).

Firemen fought to save Benney's — then demolition men knocked it down... (See page 50).

Service Medal in 1968, took an appointment as an assistant chief fire officer in the new Hampshire Fire Brigade, and his 40 years of service to the city were praised in tributes by civic dignitaries.

During its 26 years the brigade had answered 38,161 calls, of which 19,829 were to actual fires, 8,093 were to false alarms, 6,272 were chimneys, and 3,454 were special service calls. A fitting tribute to the work of the brigade on its close came in the words of the Home Secretary, Mr. Roy Jenkins in his message to the British fire service on April 1. Responsibility for the fire service was passing from those brigades which had been in being for 26 years to the new authorities taking over on that date, he said.

"I know of the skill, courage and resolution which your work demands, and I am glad to have this opportunity of thanking your all for your achievements.

"The brigades which are now ceasing to exist have served their local communities well and have enhanced the reputation of the British fire service. I am confident that the high standards achieved over the years will be maintained and improved by the new brigades."

Day to day fire cover for Portsmouth was effectively no different under amalgamation once the city was an integral part of the new Hampshire Fire Brigade. Portsmouth became the divisional headquarters of "B" division, with its administrative umbrella covering 14 stations - the three in the city together with Havant, Fareham, Gosport, Petersfield, Waterlooville, Hayling Island, Wickham, Horndean, Emsworth, Titchfield, and Portchester.

Divisional commander for the area - effectively the chief fire officer of Portsmouth under the new regime - was the late Senior Divisional Officer Bernard Harland. One major advantage of the amalgamation was said to be that the availability of a greater number of pumps would improve fire cover for the city, with surrounding pumps being sent into the city more readily in case of major fires.

Kids with fireworks played here just before Bonfire Night. Their bonfire took out the back half of the Theatre Royal (See page 50).

It didn't take long for the new system to be tested when one of Portsmouth's biggest fires for five years broke out on South Parade Pier on June 11, 1974 – a glorious sunny summer's day. Built on the remains of the earlier pier, itself destroyed by fire as we have seen in 1904, South Parade Pier had been made available to the Ken Russell film team for a sequence for a rock opera called Tommy. The blaze which received nation-wide publicity was attributed by the brigade to an arc lamp setting fire to a black velvet drape being used by the film company.

I, for my pains, in covering the fire for The News had the misfortune of catching the eye of none other than Ken Russell himself. With the pier disintegrating in great sheets of flame, and with a huge towering column of smoke filling the summer sky, I chose that moment to ask Ken what I thought was a pertinent question. As he was actually carrying a film camera across his

Portsmouth machines in action at the front of the Theatre Royal with more Hampshire appliances arriving...

Round the back, firemen getting the turntable ladder to work as the flames burst through the roof...

Now the main roof explodes as the fire reaches its height.

Courtesy The News

59

Framed between the Brigade's fire-engines, H.M.S. Victory is saved from potential disaster in 1973. (See page 50)

Courtesy The News

shoulders and filming at the time, I inquired whether he thought his outfit was in any way responsible for the outbreak. What I thought was pertinent he obviously thought was impertinent, and I ducked the swinging camera, taking the gesture to mean "no comment".

Thousands of holidaymakers watched as the flames licked up into the roof of the old wooden structure and spread furiously until three-quarters of the pier was a blazing beacon. For film-goers the blaze made spectacular footage in the final version of Tommy iself, but more interestingly for the brigade it was a useful test of how the new outfit would handle a big fire.

Within a few minutes of its outbreak, the first officers on the scene had called for six pumps, bringing all the city's appliances to action. Already – as predicted – surrounding Hampshire machines were filling in the gaps. For the next hour as the blaze, fanned by a strong sea breeze, swept through the pier, more and more calls went out for

Reaching the fire high on H.M.S. Victory's hull was a menace. Here, the turntable ladder is brought in...   *Courtesy The News*

Scrambling up ladders, in the portholes, on the deck, firemen find ways of getting at the fire on H.M.S. Victory.   *Courtesy The News*

Spectacular cinema is made as South Parade Pier is devoured by flames and smoke in the hot summer of 1974... and the film cameras kept rolling... (See page 59)

reinforcements until ultimately 15 engines were called in.

From throughout "B" division and even wider afield in southern Hampshire machines were being mobilized, first filling in empty fire stations, and then being sent on to the pier. The final tally was 18 engines moved for the fire and the brigade was reckoned to have passed its first test well. Piers have always been bad fire risks, and fighting fires on them is notoriously difficult – yet part of the landmark was saved. Within 24 hours plans were being made for the pier to be rebuilt, and it was in under a year.

The true test of integration of Portsmouth into the new county set-up came in the unprecedented fire blitz endured by Hampshire during the drought of 1976. The whole nation underwent a great ordeal by fire, and Hampshire was hit as hard as any county in the

Once gleaming-white turrets were South Parade Pier's hallmark. They soon blackened, blazed and collapsed...   *Courtesy The News*

Once the flames had the Pier's wooden roof, the south's top landmark was doomed...   *Courtesy The News*

land. Late in April Hampshire's fire chiefs were urgently imploring the county populace to beware of carelessness in the countryside – yet already the first ten and 20 pump forest and heath fires were tackled mainly in the north and the New Forest areas.

By late April, the Forestry Commission described the situation in Hampshire as the greatest threat to timber stocks this Century. May gave little respite but provided a buffer before the dreadful onslaught of fire unleashed on the county in June and July. Hampshire Fire Brigade was stretched to the very limits, dealing with 209 fires in one day, which included some wide-ranging forest conflagrations spreading like walls of fire across acres of countryside.

In the first eight days of July, Hampshire Fire Brigade answered 1,300 calls and even the city men like Portsmouth's fire-fighters were not spared. On July 11 Southsea and Copnor fire crews found themselves tackling a massive forest fire in Ringwood Forest where 30 engines from Hampshire, Dorset and Wiltshire were in action. Drought warnings were ignored by country users and the blazes spread into August without a pause.

But what befell the county on August 22 was frightening – even by the extraordinary standards the brigade was beginning to take as the new norm. Already the brigade had got used to having officers stacked up on the radio waiting to put in urgent "make-up" calls for reinforcements. Radio procedures were dramatically revised. Three quarters of all regular fire call transmissions were cut out, leaving just "assistance" and "stop" messages. They too were shortened. A coded letter system was brought in so that entire fires might be summed up in a few seconds of radio space.

August 22 was a day when the wind blew strong and hot, and when the worst possible combination developed, with many fires spreading out of control quickly and at the same time. Hampshire's fire control was getting used to mobilizing for the big fires. But here they had several fires growing simultaneously. "Make pumps four,

Film-star derelicts in Portsmouth, and film-extra rescuers in action. It was all done for the rock-opera Tommy. They're real firemen putting out the fires.   Courtesy The News

64

Shops and stores have suffered a crop of bad fires. Here, a bicycle shop at Hilsea goes up in smoke..
                                                    Courtesy The News

Horrific charred bodies after a blaze at the Tricorn in Landport? Relax, these are dress-shop dummies..
                                                    Courtesy The News

"five, eight, ten" at one fire was matched blow for blow at another.

By the height of the action the brigade was dealing with eight major fires. Three of them had reached "make pumps ten" proportions, two more were eight-pumpers, and the others were at "make pumps five". On top there were 150 smaller fires burning in the county. And on this day, the worst and biggest blaze of all was in Portsmouth.

Like many fires that year it was started by kids playing with matches. It soon spread into crates of aircraft engines stacked over acres of land on Hilsea's industrial estate. As firemen hit the crated engines with water I watched the magnesium components blow into incandescent balls of white fire – spreading the fire further. Soon it engulfed the Hants and Sussex Aviation factory. Along one boundary of the estate was a high grass embankment topped with firs, which soon became a raging forest fire.

Downwind, lost to sight in the heavy rolling smoke was the remainder of the industrial estate consisting of underground fuel dumps, factories and offices. The brigade held the fire at the downwind boundary, where men wearing breathing apparatus out in the open stopped the fire right on top of the underground tanks. Everything between them and the point where the fire started was destroyed. The factory collapsed and was burned out, and thousands of aero engines and parts just melted.

It would have been a memorable fire on its own. That day it was just one lick of fire as Hampshire burned.

Never once did the pace slacken. Late in August Hampshire dealt with another 200 fires in one day, and every day Portsmouth men were fire-fighting in Bordon, Aldershot, the New Forest and on the West Sussex borders. The daily pattern was to be called out say to Havant, deal with a fire – and then be the next nearest machine for a shout at Petersfield. With that finished the Portsmouth men would become reinforcement "make-up" material for Haslemere. On some

After the long hot summer of 1976 all that remained of the Hants and Sussex Aviation factory was twisted metal. Courtesy The News

One way to stop the traffic! A blazing derelict shop brings 'North End' evening rush-hour to a halt... Courtesy The News

66

days they were used as assistance fire-fighters in Surrey, and even fought fires in Camberley.

It all ended very abruptly in September when on the 11th the brigade was almost overwhelmed with calls to flooding as torrential rain-storms swept into the area, and parched land meant the water could not drain away.

In a few weeks the situation returned to normal. Portsmouth firemen dealt with a ten-pump fire on board the guided missile destroyer H.M.S. Kent in November which wiped out an untold number of toilet rolls in a store, and in December, a six-pump fire which took the roof of a city school was the last big fire of the year.

In the first weeks of 1977 work began on the long-awaited Southsea fire station. There was a slight hitch in March when unexploded shells were found in the gravel being used on the site, and work stopped for a few hours while they were blown up.

But not everything was well within the fire service. Throughout 1977 rumblings of industrial unrest, based on the low pay of firemen compared with the rest of industry, were heard. Last minute meetings at national level failed to bring agreement, and the Fire Brigades Union decided that on November 14 at 9 a.m. its members would strike.

Men on Portsmouth's three stations held their own meetings and decided to join the strike. At 9 a.m. on the Monday morning the men walked out. It was the first strike by firemen in history. Many of the men did not believe it would happen, and thought there would be a reprieve at one minute to nine. Many believed that having walked out and made their point they would be back inside an hour. There was a 100 per cent response from Portsmouth's men – the strongest bastion of union solidarity in Hampshire.

At 9 a.m. fire-fighting passed to the Army. For the previous few days there had been feverish activity at the fire-fighting school at H.M.S. Phoenix in Portsmouth where military personnel were given a crude crash-course in fire-fighting. Portsmouth was allocated six Green Goddesses which were engines based at H.M.S. Nelson in Queen Street, Portsea.

The Army fire-fighters had no breathing apparatus, no foam, little training – and only advisory assistance from some of Portsmouth's senior officers who were not Fire Brigade Union members. Portsmouth held its breath and waited to see how they would cope with a serious fire. None came. Two days passed before the soldiers were tested at all, when a fire in the industrial chimney of Queen Alexandra Hospital, Cosham gave them a difficult task. After four days – when some firemen were surprised to find themselves still on strike – the Army handed over fire-fighting in the city to the Royal Navy. The Army had experienced an "amazingly quiet" time

The one fire they never put out. The picket line brazier kept them warm during their coldest winter. (See page 69).   Courtesy The News

without a single big incident. Many of the crews never had a single call in their four days.

During November 18, the Navy took over the Green Goddesses and equipped with breathing apparatus and foam, they provided the city with a rather more comprehensive service.

If ever the notorious public apathy towards fire prevention propoganda needed to be overcome, it was now. And the public responded. Still no big fires troubled the military fire-fighters. The whole city became so fire conscious that fire statistics dropped like magic. On November 21, 300 firemen marched through the streets of the city and gained public support. Pickets at the three stations reported overwhelming public support, but on November 28 someone burned down the firemen's canvas lean-to at Southsea station.

Amazingly, by the end of November there had only been 33 fires in all Hampshire handled by the military. Portsmouth was described by the county's Deputy Chief Fire Officer, Mr. Arthur Tanner as the biggest risk in Hampshire, and two-thirds of the military fire-fighting incidents were in the city. But Portsmouth knew it was getting off very lightly.

Fire cover for the city was improved again on December 1 when an elite squad of highly-trained fire instructors from the Navy's fire-fighting school came on duty as a 24-hour-a-day rescue unit. Two days later, arsonists set a £10,000 blaze which damaged Hillside Middle School in Paulsgrove, but it was handled by the men in the first attendance of Green Goddesses.

By now the firemen had been out a month. They still had the general public behind them, although some were beginning to feel the real financial strain. Nevertheless, one month after the strike began, Portsmouth men voted again to reject the latest pay offer. Christmas was looming on the horizon.

Firemen dug in, knowing that their worst ever Christmas was approaching. In that cold winter I visited the men huddled round

Back to work! Soon after the strike, firemen were back in action. This transit warehouse was at Fratton. (See page 69). *Courtesy The News*

68

braziers on their picket lines every day. Passers-by would give them food parcels, and every day they would ask me if there had been any injuries from fires in the city. They were caring and unhappy men.

The Navy – usually on leave at Christmas – was preparing to be on fire-fighting duty instead. A third watch was brought in, so that by rotation of men, more would be able to get away for Christmas. Within an hour of getting "on the run" one of the new watches tackled a blaze which burned out a fourth-floor flat in a high-rise block, potentially the most dangerous yet handled by the military.

Things remained so quiet that on December 19 the elite squad was "stood down" having received not a single call. Christmas came with a final kick in the teeth for the firemen when a tax muddle robbed them of substantial sums of money. To their surprise and the nation's shock the firemen found themselves still on strike as 1978 began.

By now the men were in extreme financial difficulty and many were being forced to think about returning to work. On January 12 the Fire Brigades Union decided that the latest terms offered were good enough and the strike was called off.

On the Monday at 9 a.m. after nine painful weeks, Portsmouth's firemen went back into their stations. Their walk-in, like their walk out, was a 100 per cent response. It took two days to get the stations and machines back on top line, and on Wednesday, January 18 the Royal Navy officially stood down from their duties in Portsmouth, and the Portsmouth men of of Hampshire Fire Brigade were back "on the run".

In the nine weeks the services had answered 123 fire calls in the city – no more than an average of two a day. Not a single fire had required any reinforcements being called, and most important of all, not a single life had been lost in any fire to which the fire-fighters had been called.

The brigade went back on the run in a slightly strained atmosphere. One crew at Copnor were pitched into action immediately with a kitchen fire within two minutes of returning. Portsmouth was spared the frictions which occurred elsewhere on stations in Britain between firemen who had gone on strike and those who had not.

On January 31 the fires started again in earnest. Four engines were called to a transit warehouse near the Fratton railway goods yard – probably the biggest single building in the city outside the Dockyard. Prompt fire-fighting saved most of the building yet still thousands of pounds of damage was caused to electrical appliances in storage.

Early in the year there were major changes in the overall command of Hampshire Fire Brigade, and Portsmouth's divisional commander, the late Mr. Bernard Harland was promoted to become one of Hampshire's assistant chief officers in charge of training.

Portsmouth's new divisional commander and effective chief officer was Senior Divisional Officer George Clark, who had then served 26 years in the fire service in the city. During 1978 there were three major fires, two of which were set by arsonists – reflecting the disturbing trend of increasing numbers of deliberate fires throughout Britain in recent years.

On March 10 crews turned out to the Tesco supermarket at the Tricorn, found a first-floor storeroom heavily smoke-logged, and ten pumps were called for. Every available fireman in the city was in action together with nearly 30 more from surrounding towns. Night club revellers had to be evacuated from a club nearby, damage was set at £100,000, and later a man was jailed for three years for starting the blaze.

Another expensive fire broke out in mid-summer. June 24 was a hot Saturday – especially hot for the firemen who pulled in at an aircraft components factory on the Airport estate to find it well alight. Once again, every city fireman was called in, and the full eight-pump make-up was completed by reinforcements from outside the city. Expensive aero-engine parts were salvaged, but others worth thousands were lost, and the building badly damaged.

The last big fire of the year was again the work of a fire-raiser. During the night of October 12, crews arrived at a social club housed in a heavy old-fashioned brick building on Whale Island to find naval ratings already fire-fighting with fears that a man was lost inside. Again eight pumps were summoned, and only the good liaison between the brigade and the navy saved the building – although the club was burned out. A rating was later convicted of starting the blaze.

Years of planning and striving to replace the 32-year-old "temporary" Southsea fire station finally came to fruition. On November 7, 1978 the new long-awaited station was officially opened with the splendour and ceremony well befitting such a historical moment for the city. The £400,000 station, lavish, extensive, comfortable and futuristically designed to house six appliances, was the show-piece of all stations throughout Hampshire. City links with the Royal Navy were acknowledged when the opening was performed by Rear-Admiral Wilfred Graham, the television-star Flag Officer of Portsmouth, seen regularly in the navy's television documentary that was earning rave reviews at the time.

Portsmouth's Divisional Commander Clark was in charge of the day's drills and displays – heightened by a real fire call to a derelict house just beyond the station wall, and visible to the assembled throng.

Many of the city's former firemen and their families used the day for a grand reunion. The new station had been talked of, planned, scheduled and programmed for more than 30 years, and with its opening the city's fire-fighting capabilities were sharpened to top-line efficiency.

Trying to save people's homes. Here, on the roof in Northern Parade, Hilsea...

Hampshire Fire Brigade's mobilization scheme, which pushed reinforcement fire-engines into the city when needed, also continued to work in reverse, and Portsmouth's fire crews were often used as back-up reinforcements for big fires elsewhere in the south.

In August 1978 Portsmouth crews turned out from Cosham and Copnor to see a huge column of smoke rising in the east, showing them where they were needed as Woolworth's store at Bognor Regis blazed. They were among the 30 engines called to this blaze, which so devastated the store that it was later demolished.

City crews did not have so far to run for the next huge blaze four months later on December 8 when calls for reinforcements at South

Here, going in with breathing apparatus in Brompton Road, Southsea...

Courtesy *The News*

Downs College at Purbrook took most of Portsmouth's engines. With the top floor and roof of the complex ablaze it took nearly 100 fire-fighters manning 16 appliances to bring it under control, but not before £1,000,000 worth of damage had been caused.

And on May 3, 1979 five Portsmouth crews were part of the enormous army of 120 men mobilized in 25 machines to tackle a worrying blaze at the Ralli Bondite chemical factory in Waterlooville. Many of the crews were called in when 57 people, mostly firemen, but with press men among them, were taken to hospital after it was discovered they had breathed in isocyanate fumes enshrouding the factory. None of them was seriously affected.

In Portsmouth itself, the social menace of arson continued to flourish, giving fire-crews some of their biggest fires and escalating the fire loss figures.

Nothing is sacred to the fire-raiser, and on December 4, 1979 an arsonist struck at the Roman Catholic Cathedral in Portsmouth. Luckily a passing police woman raised the alarm early, and city fire-fighters got to grips with the blaze before it swept into the structure of the cathedral. Despite their prompt work, the damage in the sacristy totalled £20,000.

Six months later, on June 27, 1980, fire crews arrived at the Portsmouth, Gosport and District Builders Guild offices in Kingston Road, Fratton to find a fierce blaze tearing through the offices – and to be told that children were feared trapped inside. A large-scale search by six separate teams of men in breathing apparatus working in punishing conditions of heat and smoke established the building was empty. But detectives later proved that someone had been in there, and had started the fire. Another £80,000 was added to the fire losses.

Almost a year later to the week arsonists were again at work when the Motorists Discount Store in Fratton Road went up in flames. Every available city fire-fighter was in action in a desperate and successful attempt to stop flames spreading into a heavily-stocked tile warehouse next door, and to the Co-op offices on the floor above. Bursting oil cans made matters worse by splattering flowing oil into the street, making it difficult to stand up – let alone fight the fire.

And that great social evil – kids with matches – was behind the next huge blaze on October 18, 1982 when the derelict Classic Cinema in Albert Road, Southsea went up. Here was the Theatre Royal all over again. A large former house of entertainment lying derelict, a controversy about the building's future, a pair of kids playing with fire, and an arduous battle for firemen.

Its first customers had watched Vanity Fair for 3d on its first night in 1912 when it was called the Apollo Kinematic Theatre, and since November, 1975, when its last customers watched a kung-fu epic, it had lain empty.

Once flames took hold of its roof not even 30 fire-fighters with five engines and the city's hydraulic platform could save it. The roof crashed in, and damage was assessed at £500,000 making it one of the ten most expensive fires in Britain during the month.

Copnor's divisional fire headquarters, completely modernized in 1975. (See page 55).

Courtesy Simon Rowley

Southsea's new fire station, opened in 1978.

Courtesy Simon Rowley

Cosham's fire station, opened in 1952. (See page 38)

Courtesy Simon Rowley

Schools are favourite targets for arsonists. Cosham firemen helped fight this one at Cowplain.

Courtesy The News

Hazardous work for men inside the Co-op at North End. Fire rages above their heads, charred timbers beneath their feet. (See page 71)

74

Into the inferno steps another fire-fighter at first floor level...

Courtesy The News

*Up ladders and off the hydraulic platform firemen battle to stop the
Co-op blaze spreading.*

Courtesy The News

The fireball just took off the roof. It was the fumes that put 57 in hospital.
(See page 71).

But not all fires were started deliberately, and even without fire-raisers Portsmouth's firemen had some busy spells in the 1980's. They won't forget the night of January 3, 1981 quickly, for Portsmouth firemen were tackling three big fires at once that night. Most of the crews were at the Eastern Road where a blazing garage was making a spectacular bonfire. Flames had licked up from a huge stack of tyres, and the wind had fanned them into the garage itself. Once the fire was out, there was nothing left but to demolish the ruins and rebuild from scratch.

Not far away, at Langstone to the east, Portsmouth crews were providing back-up for Havant's men tackling a large blaze in the I.B.M. sports and social club, and another Portsmouth crew was elsewhere in Havant fighting a barn blaze which destroyed several buildings and 20,000 bales of hay.

At the end of June, 1982 Divisional Commander Clark retired after a distinguished career that included earning the B.E.M. The city was then served by three more divisional commanders in the 1980's. Mr. Clark's place was taken by Divisional Commander Malcolm Eastwood, who was the city's effective chief fire officer from June 1982 until October 1984. When he was promoted, Divisional Commander Ian Crosfield took over, sharing the command with his deputy, Divisional Officer Roy Derham. In June 1985, Portsmouth's new fire commander was Senior Divisional Officer Alban Barrett, who maintains the post today.

August 1983 brought back memories of the 1976 heatwave spell, and for a few weeks Portsmouth firemen fought their share of forest and heathland fires. Once again, the public chose to ignore warnings about the "tinder-box" state of the countryside, and on several days Hampshire Fire Brigade dealt with 100 fires a day. Cosham's crews spent most of their time working to combat heathland fires across Portsdown Hill.

Three big fires were tackled in 1984, with the biggest paralysing the centre of North End for half a day. A dawn call on July 17 brought

Copnor's first crews to the old disused Co-op store at North End junction.

They were met by an astonishing sight. Great tongues of flame were leaping from the first floor clear across the main London Road, and cracking windows of shops on the other side. Every city fire-fighter was called in, plus many Hampshire crews, until 70 men were in the battle using 13 engines.

North End was under real threat. Adjoining the disused store was a large food hall immediately in the path of the flames. Intense heat across the road was threatening shops and stores, and at roof level, flames were almost brushing the upper floors of a night club.

For the first hour, firemen concentrated on stopping the spread to any other buildings, then, with that threat removed, they spent the rest of the day dousing the blaze inside the giant corner block. Its roof collapsed, and the final damage was put at £700,000.

This blaze was sandwiched between two others which brought untold heartache to Southsea's flats and bedsit land. On July 10, just a week before the North End inferno, 30 city fire-fighters were called to Western Parade where a roof blaze had sent workmen scuttling to safety down scaffolding as the fire took hold. Working off the city's hydraulic platform, firemen confined the blaze to the top floor and roof, and no-one was endangered.

It was a different story on the night of October 14, when a blaze swept through the upper floors and roof of a block of flats in Clarence Parade, Southsea, and at least 50 people were very much endangered. Two women endured a terrifying walk along the sloping roof of the building away from the flames. Others escaped down ladders from smoke-filled rooms, and soon charred timbers and masonry was crashing down into the fire-ravaged wreckage of the building.

All Portsmouth's fire-fighters were there, with Hampshire reinforcements until 70 men were in action, manning 13 fire engines. Their task was hopeless. When the fire was out 66 people were homeless, and the damage was put at £150,000. The Lord Mayor donated from his charity appeal to a fund to help the homeless, and a large-scale rehousing operation was launched.

Sadly, it seemed that some of the unfortunates displaced by the fire took the jinx with them. On June 30, 1985, eight months later, firemen were called to a block of flats in Lion Terrace, Portsea, and some of the rehoused homeless were burned out again. This time every fire-engine in the city was sent, and the blaze was confined to the top floor and roof. But 16 flats were damaged and 23 tenants were made homeless.

Firemen figured in a dreadful murder in the city in March, 1985 when they were called early on a Sunday morning to the Vernon public house ablaze in Flathouse Road by the city's commercial docklands. Upstairs in the fiercely burning pub it was men in breathing apparatus who found the body of the much-loved landlord with his throat slit.

A cold-blooded intruder had been burgling the pub, had knifed the landlord to death in his bed, then set it on fire, setting another fire downstairs, hoping to destroy the whole pub and cover his crime. But the city firemen put out the blaze, enabling enough evidence to be found to trap the killer. Nearly a year later, early in 1986, a German seaman from a ship berthed that night not a hundred yards from the pub was jailed for life for the murderous attack.

Portsmouth in the 1980's is protected by as efficient a fire-fighting force as it has ever had. The only constant factor in all the years of change over the Centuries is that there will always be fires. Any fire officer will tell you that people cause fires, and people never learn. There will always be another fire tomorrow.

Quick, call the brigade! The next fire breaks out in the city, and you can be sure there will always be a "next" one.